WHAT PRINCIPALS NEED TO KNOW ABOUT

Teaching and Learning Mathematics

TIMOTHY D. KANOLD

DIANE J. BRIARS

FRANCIS (SKIP) FENNELL

A Joint Publication

naesp

Solution Tree

555 North Morton Street
Bloomington, IN 47404
800.733.6786 (toll free) / 812.336.7700
FAX: 812.336.7790

email: info@solution-tree.com
solution-tree.com

Visit **go.solution-tree.com/leadership** to download the reproducibles for this book.

Printed in the United States of America

15 14 13 12   2 3 4 5

Library of Congress Cataloging-in-Publication Data

Kanold, Timothy D.
  What principals need to know about teaching and learning mathematics / Timothy D. Kanold, Diane J. Briars, Frances (Skip) Fennell.
        p. cm.
  Includes bibliographical references and index.
  ISBN 978-1-935543-55-8 (perfect bound) -- ISBN 978-1-935543-56-5 (library edition) 1. Mathematics--Study and teaching (Elementary) 2. Elementary school principals. I. Briars, Diane Jane, 1951- II. Fennell, Francis M., 1944- III. Title.
  QA135.6.K365 2012
  372.7--dc23
                          2011036897

Solution Tree
Jeffrey C. Jones, CEO & President

Solution Tree Press
President: Douglas M. Rife
Publisher: Robert D. Clouse
Vice President of Production: Gretchen Knapp
Managing Production Editor: Caroline Wise
Copy Editor: Rachel Rosolina
Text and Cover Designer: Jenn Taylor

To Lee E. Yunker, who died way too young, left his leadership imprint on many, and taught me how to become a mathematics education leader. —Timothy D. Kanold

To Jim—for your loving support and intellectual challenges that enhance my work every day. —Diane J. Briars

To Quinn, Griffin, Chase, Paige, Cameron, Mia, Bryce, Bree, and Cooper—for making me think hard every day about mathematics teaching and learning. —Francis (Skip) Fennell

ACKNOWLEDGMENTS

Solution Tree Press would like to thank the following reviewers:

Susie Black
Principal
McAlder Elementary School
Puyallup, Washington

Aaron C. Brewer
Principal
Mexican Hat Elementary School
Blanding, Utah

Juli K. Dixon
Professor, Mathematics Education
University of Central Florida
Orlando, Florida

Shirley Frye
Retired Mathematics Educator
Former NCTM President
Cave Creek, Arizona

Jessica Kanold-McIntyre
Principal
Aptakisic Junior High School
Buffalo Grove, Illinois

Mike Roth
Principal
Turman Elementary School
Colorado Springs, Colorado

Barbara Rudiak
Assistant Superintendent, K–5 Schools
Pittsburgh Public Schools
Pittsburgh, Pennsylvania

Denise A. Spangler
Professor, Department of Mathematics and
  Science Education
University of Georgia
Athens, Georgia

Michael D. Steele
Assistant Professor, Department of Teacher
  Education
Michigan State University
East Lansing, Michigan

Carolyn Lee Taylor
Assistant Superintendent, Curriculum and
  Instruction
Mobile County Public Schools
Mobile, Alabama

Mark Thames
Assistant Research Scientist, School of
  Education
University of Michigan
Ann Arbor, Michigan

TABLE OF CONTENTS

ABOUT THE AUTHORS

Timothy D. Kanold, PhD, is the former director of mathematics and science and also served as superintendent of Adlai E. Stevenson High School District 125, a model professional learning community district in Lincolnshire, Illinois. Dr. Kanold is founder and director of E²-PLC Learning Group. He conducts professional development leadership seminars worldwide with a focus on systematic change initiatives that create and sustain greater equity, access, and success for all students. Dr. Kanold was a member of the writing teams for the *Professional Standards for Teaching Mathematics* (2001), he helped revise the *Professional Standards for Teaching Mathematics* (2009), and he was lead editor for the *Principles and Indicators for Mathematics Education* leadership framework. He is a former president of the National Council of Supervisors of Mathematics.

Dr. Kanold has authored numerous articles and chapters on school leadership for education publications, including the *Journal of Staff Development* and the *School Administrator*. He received a bachelor's degree in education and a master's degree in mathematics from Illinois State University and earned a doctorate in educational leadership and philosophy from Loyola University Chicago. He is the author of *The Five Disciplines of PLC Leaders*.

To learn more about Dr. Kanold's work, visit his blog Turning Vision Into Action at tkanold .blogspot.com or follow @tkanold or #plcleaders on Twitter.

Diane J. Briars, PhD, is a mathematics education consultant and is codirector of the Algebra Intensification Project, an NSF-supported design-based research project to support underprepared algebra students. Previously, she served for twenty years as mathematics director for the Pittsburgh Public Schools. Under her leadership, Pittsburgh schools made significant progress in increasing student achievement through standards-based curricula, instruction, and assessment. Dr. Briars was a member of the writing team for the *Curriculum and Evaluation Standards* and the *Professional Standards for Assessing Mathematics*.

Dr. Briars is also involved in national initiatives in mathematics education. She has served as a member of many committees, including the National

Commission of Mathematics and Science Teaching for the 21st Century headed by Senator John Glenn. She is a former president of the National Council of Supervisors of Mathematics and board member for the National Council of Teachers of Mathematics, and she has served in leadership roles for other organizations, including the College Board and the National Science Foundation. She earned a PhD in mathematics education and her master's and bachelor's degrees in mathematics from Northwestern University, and she did postdoctoral study in the Psychology Department of Carnegie-Mellon University. She began her career as a secondary mathematics teacher.

Francis (Skip) Fennell, PhD, is a mathematics educator and has experience as a classroom teacher, principal, and supervisor of instruction. He is the initial recipient of the L. Stanley Bowlsbey endowed chair as Professor of Education and Graduate and Professional Studies at McDaniel College in Westminster, Maryland, where he has served for thirty-six years. He is a recent past president of the National Council of Teachers of Mathematics (NCTM). Dr. Fennell also currently directs the Brookhill Foundation–supported *Elementary Mathematics Specialists and Teacher Leaders Project*, which includes a national clearinghouse for elementary school mathematics specialists. Dr. Fennell was a member of the writing teams for the *Principles and Standards for School Mathematics*, *Curriculum Focal Points*, and the *Common Core State Standards*. Dr. Fennell also served as a member of the National Mathematics Advisory Panel from 2006 to 2008.

Dr. Fennell is widely published in professional journals and textbooks related to elementary and middle grade mathematics education and has also authored chapters in yearbooks and resource books. In addition, he has played key leadership roles with NCTM, the Research Council for Mathematics Learning, the Mathematical Sciences Education Board, the National Science Foundation, the Maryland Mathematics Commission, the United States National Commission for Mathematics Instruction, and the Association for Mathematics Teacher Educators. He earned his bachelor's degree from Lock Haven University of Pennsylvania and his PhD from The Pennsylvania State University.

To book Tim, Diane, or Skip for professional development, contact pd@solution-tree.com.

INTRODUCTION
EXPECTATIONS IN MATHEMATICS EDUCATION

Knowing mathematics is important! Why is it that this subject sends a "nerd-alert" signal even at the elementary school level? Those who actually wore pocket protectors and truly value mathematics find this inexcusable, particularly at a time when we want—make that *need*—a much greater proportion of our citizenry to be prepared for careers in the fields of science, technology, engineering, and mathematics. Elementary and middle school is the time to engage students in doing mathematics and also to plant the seed of mathematics importance. Young children begin their schooling seemingly loving math; they enjoy number-related adventures and like to play with shapes. They also see connections to mathematics learning as they engage in the myriad of organized activities that appear to invade and extend their school day. Students see and hear connections like "let's divide into three teams, angle the ball, hit the cutoff man, pass along the diagonal, find the slugging percentage," and on and on.

Mathematics can, and frankly *must*, make a difference in the lives of children at the elementary and middle grade levels, and we—all of us—must take advantage of this opportunity. As you move toward implementation of the Common Core State Standards (CCSS), engaging the Mathematical Practices that the CCSS define will help guide the mathematics content domain experiences that form the foundation so critical for further mathematics learning.

As an elementary school principal, assistant principal, or school-based mathematics instructional leader, your mathematics teaching and learning responsibilities can be difficult challenges. In particular, leading mathematics teaching and learning involves understanding and following policy issues unique to the content area. It is undeniable that the public school system is a social institution influenced by policy at the district, state, and federal levels, and we must acknowledge and respect how the social context of the school impacts mathematics teaching and learning.

Policy Expectations

The CCSS represent, for the first time in U.S. history, a set of common expectations for grades K–12. The CCSS have the potential to significantly affect and shift the day-to-day teaching paradigms of elementary school teachers.

The Common Core State Standards for mathematics define what students should understand and be able to do in mathematics in order to be college and career ready by the end of grade 12. Created by a writing team that included mathematicians, mathematics educators, teachers, and mathematics leaders, they provide expectations that strive to develop understanding of and proficiency in important mathematics topics (Council of Chief State School Officers, 2010a). This historic initiative was driven by the National Governors Association and the Council of Chief State School Officers (CCSSO), which maintains the Common Core State Standards website (www.corestandards.org). At the time of this publication, forty-five states have adopted the CCSS and are moving forward in their transitions toward classroom implementation, with the goal that by the 2014–2015 school year, the United States will have a common set of mathematics standards for all students. The potential of this initiative is both challenging and historic.

As we move toward a deeper discussion of mathematics curriculum, instruction, and assessment, we will continuously circle back to these standards.

The appraisal tool in table I.1 provides a way for you to examine the CCSS mathematical content domains and to consider how they relate to your school's readiness, ranging from the teachers' content backgrounds to their understanding of the developmental learning issues related to each of the content domains, as well as to domain-based instructional needs regarding planning, teaching, and assessment. For instance, given the importance of fractions in grades 3–5, it would make sense to consider a professional development focus on fractions developmentally, beginning at the first-grade level with expectations such as:

> Partition circles and rectangles into two and four equal shares, describe the shares using the words halves, fourths, and quarters, and use the phrases half of, fourth of, and quarter of. Describe the whole as two of, or four of the shares. Understand for these examples that decomposing into more equal shares creates smaller shares. (CCSSO, 2010a, p. 16)

While understanding fractions is an important component of mathematics learning at the middle grade levels, the depth of understanding must occur at the elementary level. Do your grade-level teachers understand the critical importance of this grade 1 expectation? Is the content background of your teachers sufficient to expand the standard for advanced students and consider the prerequisites for students who may not be ready for this particular slice of mathematics at the first-grade level?

While the fraction analysis example is standard specific, domain-by-domain analysis using table I.1 is a likely first step in a professional development session. Teachers could suggest their own readiness levels using *yes* or *no,* or the school's administrative and mathematics teacher

Table I.1: CCSS Needs Assessment for Mathematics Content, Learning, and Instructional Needs

CCSS Mathematics Domains	Content Grade Level(s)	Content Needs (yes/no)	Developmental Learning Needs (yes/no)	Instructional Needs: Planning (yes/no)	Instructional Needs: Teaching (yes/no)	Instructional Needs: Assessment (yes/no)
Counting and Cardinality	K (only)					
Operations and Algebraic Thinking	K–5					
Number and Operations—Base Ten	K–5					
Number and Operations—Fractions	3–5 (only)					
Measurement and Data	K–5					
Geometry	K–8					
Ratios and Proportional Relationships	6, 7 (only)					
The Number System	6–8					
Expressions and Equations	6–8					
Functions	8 (only)					
Statistics and Probability	6–8					

*Visit **go.solution-tree.com/leadership** for a reproducible version of this table.*

leader could use the table to define the school's needs related to particular areas of content emphasis within the CCSS. The table provides a means to consider *your* current reality. It is certainly a needs-assessment tool but can also be used to monitor implementation and to update your school's progress on the path toward full CCSS implementation.

The transition to implementation of the CCSS will include use of one of two consortia assessments. At this writing, twenty-four states have indicated an interest in implementing the Partnership for Assessment of Readiness for College and Careers (PARCC) Assessments, and thirty states have signed on to consider use of the SMARTER Balanced Assessments. Note that the total of states expressing interest in the PARCC *and* SMARTER balanced assessments is greater than the number of states agreeing to implement the Common Core State Standards. This total represents several states that, at present, are considering both assessment plans, realizing that they will need to determine which assessment they will actually use by 2014. The development of both the PARCC and SMARTER balanced assessments is supported by funding from the U.S. Department of Education. Initial assessments are planned for the 2013–2014 school year. Full implementation of these No Child Left Behind replacement assessments for grades 3–8 and high school will occur during the 2014–2015 school year.

The seemingly simultaneous transition and implementation of the CCSS followed by either the PARCC or SMARTER balanced assessments is a significant policy-related challenge for principals. Specific issues will include how this curriculum and related assessment changes will affect teacher observation and evaluation procedures. What can be done to strengthen a school's mathematics academic profile while also ensuring a challenging mathematics learning experience for an increasingly diverse student population? While the social forces of educational policy may impact daily challenges and work, they also serve to emphasize that the changes you consider must be grounded in addressing the importance of effective mathematics content, learning, instruction, and assessment.

The issues of equity and access must also become important considerations for mathematics education. To ensure a challenging mathematics experience for every learner, every day, principals must find ways to support and encourage improved mathematics achievement and to develop positive adult and student dispositions at each grade level.

Teacher Teams

As principal, one of the most effective moves in the transition toward implementation of the CCSS is to require teachers to work on mathematics instruction in collaborative grade-level and cross-level teams. Such teams are discussed throughout this text. Three tasks are necessary to institute grade-level and cross-level collaborative planning: (1) create a schedule that includes regular grade-level and cross-level planning time; (2) set explicit expectations about how to use this planning time, as well as what products should result; and (3) monitor the collaborative work.

Teams should focus on content domain planning. Specifically, for each domain, every grade-level or cross-level team should do the following:

- Understand and agree on major learning goals of a particular topic (such as place value) and the expected degree of student proficiency on the CCSS learning targets and standards.

- Develop common end-of-topic emphasis assessments.

- Analyze or select high-level tasks to engage core concepts or skills for the mathematical topic. (Ideally, such tasks are already in the team's instructional materials. If not, teachers will need to find or develop such tasks collaboratively, which is much more efficient than doing this in isolation.)

- Create detailed lesson plans to support the implementation of high-level tasks using the CCSS Mathematical Practices (detailed further in appendix A on page 107).

- Debrief implementation of the high-level task lessons. What did the students do? What unexpected responses came up? What went well? What challenges did the students confront?

- Analyze results of the topic's assessment by discussing how well students achieved the topic goals overall, what instructional modifications are needed for next year, and which individual students need additional support on specific concepts or skills now.

The principal must establish a monitoring and accountability mechanism regarding these expectations. It is important to establish a feedback mechanism to monitor the progress of the grade-level teams. If you have a mathematics specialist or instructional leader, this individual could meet regularly with the grade-level and cross-level teams, as appropriate.

Chapter Summaries

The first four chapters each focus on one aspect of a high-quality mathematics program: content, instruction, assessment, and response to intervention. Each of these chapters includes a section on the research informing that topic. The last four chapters look more closely at the overarching concepts of evaluation, professional development, family engagement, and taking action. All chapters include a section on priorities related to that topic.

Chapter 1, "High-Quality Mathematics Content," answers the question, What mathematical knowledge will teachers need relative to the proposed curriculum changes within the CCSS? This chapter also discusses learning trajectories as related to CCSS progressions and introduces the CCSS Mathematical Practices. As states and school districts transition to the vision of the CCSS, you will need to prioritize needs concerning the content knowledge of your staff. Should you focus on professional development related to fractions first? Would it make more sense to work on place value across all grades? These kinds of questions will push the prioritization process.

Chapter 2, "High-Quality Mathematics Instruction," addresses the need to identify and analyze concerns specifically related to instruction. You must consider how staff will access and use a variety of instructional tools that will help students develop critical mathematics concepts and skills as well as develop the "habits of mind" and dispositions—the CCSS Mathematical Practices, per se—that will enable them to use mathematics effectively. This chapter also discusses the importance of eight specific instructional strategies that will promote teacher action in the expectations and the vision of the CCSS Mathematical Practices—especially concerning the role of student formative feedback and how to promote students' positive self-beliefs.

Chapter 3, "High-Quality Mathematics Assessment," uses a five-step assessment cycle to delineate how staff can collaborate to build proficiency using a variety of formative and summative mathematics assessments. The highly effective principal understands that *assessment* is no longer defined by and limited to the summative function of unit assessments.

Chapter 4, "High-Quality Mathematics Response to Intervention," will help guide decisions about developing and implementing intervention programs in classroom and Tier 3–type pull-out programs. It specifically discusses the role of response to intervention (RTI) in mathematics. Teachers who understand how children learn are able to establish environments that support individual and collaborative learning and to actively engage their students in the learning of mathematics.

Chapter 5, "Monitoring, Evaluating, and Improving Instruction," discusses how to use the observation-conferring-reflection cycle to improve each teacher's mathematics instruction and to ensure equity of learning opportunities for all students. This chapter also addresses how to use elementary mathematics specialists, academic coaches, or teacher leaders to promote schoolwide improvements in mathematics instruction.

Chapter 6, "Designing Effective Professional Development," details effective design and use of collaborative teacher teams as part of ongoing professional development. It is necessary for principals to determine how they and, if available, a school-based mathematics specialist, instructional leader, or academic coach can engage all faculty members and other critical staff in improved instructional practice. Like students in the classrooms, teachers feel engaged and supported when they are free to discuss concerns, admit challenges, and try something different.

Chapter 7, "Working With Families," examines the diversity of families and how it affects mathematics teaching and learning. This chapter also recommends different ways you can engage and involve families in the mathematics program, such as math nights, parent-teacher conferences, and math newsletters, and highlights resources to support parents and caregivers working with their children outside of school.

Chapter 8, "Turning the Mathematics Vision Into Action," presents guiding questions for developing a highly successful mathematics program in your school. It also discusses the importance of setting priorities, distributing ownership, and celebrating.

This book asks principals to frame the mathematics needs and challenges faced at the school and district levels around content, learning, and instructional expectations. The following chapters take an in-depth look at the principal's role regarding essential elements in mathematics curriculum, learning, instruction, and assessment. The discussion includes practice- and research-informed insights into the important issues affecting and shaping the field of mathematics education. Visit **go.solution-tree.com/leadership** for chapter-by-chapter "Digging Deeper" lists of more resources.

ONE

HIGH-QUALITY MATHEMATICS CONTENT

As schools and districts transition to the vision of the Common Core State Standards (CCSS), principals must consider what content issues to address in the mathematics curriculum. Looking at high-quality mathematics, they must also understand which essential elements and expectations are taught in their school, as well as how they know they're being taught.

This chapter focuses on issues involving mathematics content and, to a lesser extent, instructional practices as part of the overall content development. It begins with one of the most important content paradigm shifts of CCSS expectations: drilling deeper into content development and student understanding. At every grade level, faculty will teach fewer mathematics content standards. However, teachers will need to "dig deeper" into each standard as they teach for conceptual understanding and skill proficiency.

Research That Informs Content

As you consider the mathematical content needs and priorities at the school level, there are a number of resources that provide the research and best practices to guide and validate decisions related to the content priorities for your students, the development progressions of particular content domains, and the mathematical knowledge your teachers will need to ease your school's implementation of the CCSS.

As a first step, consider a review of the mathematics content, learning, and instructional recommendations from the *Principles and Standards for School Mathematics* (NCTM, 2000). Existing state mathematics standards were either developed or revised based on the *Principles and Standards for School Mathematics*. The more recent Curriculum Focal Points (NCTM, 2006) were intended for states, school districts, and local schools to begin a discussion around the focus topics in grades K–8. The Curriculum Focal Points provide excellent content insight, particularly since they are, in essence, the critical topics that introduce each grade level's content discussion within the CCSS.

An important research-based resource to help guide your transition and implementation of the CCSS is the National Research Council's *Adding It Up* (NRC, 2001). This well-respected resource examines the research related to K–8 mathematics teaching and learning and is a reliable source of authority for any school-based mathematics instructional leader.

As you consider the mathematical content expertise and needs of your faculty and staff, the Conference Board of the Mathematical Sciences' *Mathematical Education of Teachers* (CBMS, 2001) will help you understand the mathematical content background of teachers at all levels and will be a useful guide as you consider teacher background and their grade-level or cross-grade teaching assignments. A 2012 edition of this work is in press.

Implementation of the CCSS will require you and your teachers to carefully consider the pace and depth of particular content domains and standards within the domains, particularly those standards that require student understanding or expect the use of a variety of representations, from manipulative materials to drawings to technological tools. *How People Learn: Brain, Mind, Experience and School* (NRC, 1999), *Mathematics Learning in Early Childhood: Paths Toward Excellence and Equity* (Cross, Woods, & Schweingruber, 2009), the work of Clements, Sarama, Spitler, Lange, and Wolfe (2011), and others will help you when considering the developmental trajectory of the mathematics concepts and skills that promote understanding and lead to fluency at particular grade levels.

Visit **go.solution-tree.com/leadership** for further resources regarding mathematics content.

Less Is More

Mathematics content helps define what teachers teach and what students learn. The CCSS organizes mathematical content according to content domains (CCSSO, 2010a), and as mentioned previously (see table I.1, page 3), one of the talking points of the Common Core State Standards is the need to focus on fewer expectations and standards per grade level.

While this "less is more" story is a good one, the reality is that teaching for conceptual understanding using a variety of instructional tools is no longer something teachers should simply consider—rather, such teaching is now a daily expectation. To illustrate, consider the following fourth-grade standard excerpt from the CCSS content domain Measurement and Data with particular attention to angles and angle measures.

Geometric Measurement: Understand Concepts of Angle and Measure Angles

5. Recognize angles as geometric shapes that are formed wherever two rays share a common endpoint, and understand concepts of angle measurement:

   a. An angle is measured with reference to a circle with its center at the common endpoint of the rays, by considering the fraction of the circular arc between the points where the two rays intersect the circle. An angle that turns through 1/360 of a circle is called a "one-degree angle," and can be used to measure angles.

    b. An angle that turns through *n* one-degree angles is said to have an angle measure of *n* degrees.

6. Measure angles in whole-number degrees using a protractor. Sketch angles of specified measure.

7. Recognize angle measure as additive. When an angle is decomposed into non-overlapping parts, the angle measure of the whole is the sum of the angle measures of the parts. Solve addition and subtraction problems to find unknown angles on a diagram in real world and mathematical problems, e.g., by using an equation with a symbol for the unknown angle measure. (CCSSO, 2010a, pp. 31–32)

This CCSS standard is deeper than many typical fourth-grade student encounters with angles, which tend to ask students to name types of angles—a low-level cognitive task. Also note that actual instructional tools and strategies are suggested as students acquire this level of understanding.

Table 1.1 shows the CCSS content domains for the K–6 mathematics curriculum. Note that the domains Operations and Algebraic Thinking, Number and Operations in Base Ten, Measurement and Data, and Geometry are elements of the elementary school mathematics curricula from kindergarten through grade 5. Also note the special attention given to the domain Counting and Cardinality at the kindergarten level and to Number and Operations—Fractions at grades 3–5.

Table 1.1: Grades K–6 Mathematics Content Domains

Kindergarten	Grades 1–2	Grades 3–5	Grade 6
Counting and Cardinality			
Operations and Algebraic Thinking	Operations and Algebraic Thinking	Operations and Algebraic Thinking	
Number and Operations in Base Ten	Number and Operations in Base Ten	Number and Operations in Base Ten	The Number System
		Number and Operations—Fractions	Ratios and Proportional Relationships
			Expressions and Equations
Measurement and Data	Measurement and Data	Measurement and Data	Statistics and Probability
Geometry	Geometry	Geometry	Geometry

*Visit **go.solution-tree.com/leadership** for a reproducible version of this table.*

Recognize, too, the departure of Operations and Algebraic Thinking, Number and Operations in Base Ten, Number and Operations—Fractions, and Measurement and Data as the mathematics "grows up" at the sixth-grade level. The content domains shift to much more of a pre-algebra focus at this level with attention to the number system, ratio and proportion, and expressions and equations. Similarly, the emphasis on data shifts from the link with measurement in grades K–5 to a specific Statistics and Probability domain beginning at grade 6. Table 1.1 shows the cross-grade compatibility of the mathematical domains from grades 1–5 and the differences in kindergarten (counting and cardinality), 3–5 (fractions), and 6 (all domains, except geometry). These considerations provide potential beginning content-topic discussions both within and across grade levels.

Table 1.2 identifies the CCSS critical topics of content focus for grades K–6. This is a different layer of mathematics analysis, targeting what's important regarding content for each grade level. Each critical area within the CCSS draws from the work of the Curriculum Focal Points (NCTM, 2006) and identifies the mathematics that must receive emphasis or focus at particular grades. These critical areas also provide emphasis topics from another perspective—yours. They highlight, for you, the topics of focus or emphasis at particular grade levels. Table 1.2 also allows you to examine your focus across grade levels. Are there topics that are critical at more than one level? Yes! You can use the focal point–related critical topics for administrative walkthroughs, faculty content and pedagogy conversations, professional development needs, and formal observation expectations.

Learning Trajectories and CCSS Progressions

It is critically important for students to understand the mathematics concepts they are learning. Conceptual understanding—understanding the *how* and *why* of mathematics—is also a requirement for teachers. Do your teachers know how to teach for understanding of the content? For instance, you should know whether your second-grade teachers are prepared to help students acquire the CCSS second-grade standard 2.NBT.9: "Explain why addition and subtraction strategies work, using place value and the properties of operations" (CCSSO, 2010a, p. 19). As principal, you are responsible for ensuring that such teacher knowledge helps identify whether students have opportunities that engage them in the learning process and instill in them procedural fluency with understanding.

The acquisition of the basic multiplication and division facts has never been unimportant. *Fluency* is defined as the student's ability to respond efficiently and accurately to tasks that involve procedures such as recall of addition and related subtraction facts; use of a standard algorithm for addition, subtraction, and multiplication; or division of whole numbers with or without fractions.

Fluency with understanding cannot be assumed, meaning that a student may be efficient and accurate in multiplying 32×45, but may not be able to explain why the product is $< 2,000$. When students truly understand, they will know that $\frac{1}{2} \times 8$ can be solved without a procedure as long as they think about $\frac{1}{2}$ of 8, or 4. The goal when working with operations is fluency with understanding. If students understand that $\frac{1}{2} \times 8$ is just finding half of 8, or 4, without a need to compute other than using mental mathematics, then understanding is connected to fluency.

Table 1.2: An Analysis of the Critical Areas in CCSS Content for Grades K–6

Kindergarten	Grade 1	Grade 2	Grade 3	Grade 4	Grade 5	Grade 6
1. Representing and comparing whole numbers, initially with sets of objects	1. Developing understanding of addition, subtraction, and strategies for addition and subtraction within 20	1. Extending understanding of base-ten notation	1. Developing understanding of multiplication and division, and strategies for multiplication and division within 100	1. Developing understanding and fluency with multidigit multiplication, and developing understanding of dividing to find quotients involving multi-digit dividends	1. Developing fluency with addition and subtraction of fractions, and developing understanding of the multiplication and division of fractions in limited cases (unit fractions divided by whole numbers and whole numbers divided by unit fractions)	1. Connecting ratio and rate to whole number multiplication and division, and using concepts of ratio and rate to solve problems
2. Describing shapes and space	2. Developing understanding of whole number relationships and place value, including grouping in tens and ones	2. Building fluency with addition and subtraction	2. Developing understanding of fractions, especially unit fractions (fractions with numerator 1)	2. Developing an understanding of fraction equivalence, addition and subtraction of fractions with like denominators, and multiplication of fractions by whole numbers	2. Extending division to two-digit divisors, integrating decimal fractions into the place value system, developing understanding of operations with decimals to hundredths, and developing fluency with whole number and decimal operations	2. Completing understanding of division of fractions and extending the notion of number to the system of rational numbers, which includes negative numbers

continued →

Kindergarten	Grade 1	Grade 2	Grade 3	Grade 4	Grade 5	Grade 6
	3. Developing understanding of linear measurement and measuring lengths as iterating units	3. Using standard units of measure	3. Developing understanding of the structure of rectangular arrays and of area	3. Understanding that geometric figures can be analyzed and classified based on their properties, such as having parallel sides, perpendicular sides, particular angle measures, and symmetry	3. Developing understanding of volume	3. Writing, interpreting, and using expressions and equations
	4. Reasoning about attributes of and composing and decomposing geometric shapes	4. Describing and analyzing shapes	4. Describing and analyzing two-dimensional shapes			4. Developing understanding of statistical thinking

*Visit **go.solution-tree.com/leadership** for a reproducible version of this table.*

In addition to general research on learning, and specific mathematics learning, there is a rich body of research about how children learn specific mathematics content and the instruction needed to support it. Three of the best sources for summaries of this research include *Adding It Up* (NRC, 2001), the *Second Handbook of Research on Mathematics Teaching and Learning* (Lester, 2007), and *Mathematics Learning in Early Childhood* (Cross et al., 2009).

Researchers have begun to develop learning trajectories (Clements et al., 2011; Confrey, 2008), sometimes called *teaching-learning paths* (Cross et al., 2009), that describe sequences of milestones children typically follow in learning particular mathematics content (such as whole numbers or basic operations). The CCSS used such pathways as the basis for the standards progression—that is, the order in which the standards appear across grades, as well as the standards that should appear together in the same grade.

A core research finding across specific topics is that conceptual understanding facilitates the acquisition of procedural fluency. Thus the CCSS standards progression for the different content domains: (1) develop conceptual understanding, often building on children's informal knowledge; (2) support conceptual knowledge and develop informal strategies to solve problems within the domain; and (3) refine the informal strategies to develop fluency with standard procedures.

This progression—conceptual understanding to informal strategies to fluency—poses a significant paradigm shift in teaching mathematics for some teachers. In particular, three progressions in the CCSS content domains that differ significantly from current practice are the domains Operations and Algebraic Thinking, Number and Operations in Base Ten, and Number and Operations—Fractions. Faculty will need to be prepared for these changes. In some cases, the changes will be greater emphasis on topics within domains. In other cases, topics that were presented as expectations at a particular grade will be presented earlier. Examples are fractions being more prominent and extended in grades 3–5 and probability not being introduced until grade 7. Another change is the use of representations (for example, base-ten blocks, fraction models, and the number line) to build and extend concepts. The use of such representations is spelled out in the CCSS, and students are expected to use representations (from manipulatives to drawings to technical tools) throughout their quest for understanding key mathematical concepts. These CCSS content domains and the role of varied representations are prime targets for grade-level or school-based professional development.

The content progressions for addition/subtraction and multiplication/division of whole numbers are similar. They begin by providing students opportunities to engage conceptually using informal methods—counting, acting out, drawing pictures, and so forth. They then progress to writing number sentences using the operations symbols and developing more formal strategies for solving problems.

This important sequencing has two major elements:

1. Instruction starts with solving problems and building meaning and understanding of the operations rather than "teaching" the operations out of context first, and then solving word problems as applications.

2. Students work with a wide variety of addition/subtraction and multiplication/division situations, not just ones in which the result is unknown. This will be an important difference for many teachers (see tables 1 and 2, CCSSO, 2010a, pp. 88–89).

The progression to developing computational proficiency with a standard algorithm for the four basic operations is a historic and important outcome of elementary school mathematics. For each operation, students first build conceptual understanding of the operation and the properties and relationships of the operation; students then have several years to develop proficiency with strategies they can justify. Expected proficiency with standard algorithms for addition and subtraction (grade 4), multiplication (grade 5), and division (grade 6) is on a multiyear trajectory to provide students time to develop understandings of why and how these related, but different procedures work.

CCSS Mathematical Practices

One of the more important contributions of the 2010 Common Core State Standards is the Mathematical Practices. These rest on the process standards of *Principles and Standards for School Mathematics* (PSSM; NCTM, 2000) and are the strands of mathematical proficiency specified in *Adding It Up* (NRC, 2001). They describe additional content expertise that all teachers must seek as students develop mathematical competence in procedural knowledge and ability to demonstrate understanding. The Mathematical Practices describe ways in which students are to be actively doing mathematics.

Table 1.3 highlights the interrelatedness of the NCTM Process Standards (NCTM, 2000), mathematical proficiency as defined in *Adding It Up* (NRC, 2001), and the Common Core's Mathematical Practices. Together they suggest how teachers should consider *how* students are to engage in mathematics learning. Four important proficiency-related considerations expect students to regularly experience mathematics that will nurture and develop reasoning, problem solving, conceptual understanding, and a productive disposition. *Adding It Up* (NRC, 2001) defines *productive disposition* as "having the inclination to see mathematics as sensible, useful, and worthwhile, coupled with a belief in diligence and one's own efficacy" (p. 5). As students grow mathematically, every teacher's goal should be to nurture a student's productive disposition.

Table 1.3: Relating the Standards for Mathematical Practice (CCSS) to Strands of Mathematical Proficiency (*Adding It Up*) and the Process Standards (NCTM)

Adding It Up—Mathematical Proficiency	CCSS—Mathematical Practices	PSSM—Process Standards
Strategic competence	Make sense of problems and persevere in solving them.	Problem solving
Adaptive reasoning	Reason abstractly and quantitatively.	Reasoning and proof
Conceptual understanding, procedural fluency, adaptive reasoning	Construct viable arguments and critique the reasoning of others.	Reasoning and proof, communication
Conceptual understanding, strategic competence	Model with mathematics.	Connections
Conceptual understanding	Use appropriate tools strategically.	Representation
Procedural fluency, strategic competence	Attend to precision.	Communication
Procedural fluency	Look for and make use of structure.	Communication, representation
Adaptive reasoning	Look for and express regularity in repeated reasoning.	Reasoning and Proof
Productive disposition		

Source: CCSSO, 2010a; NRC, 2001; NCTM, 2000.

Table 1.4 (page 18) presents the Mathematical Practices of the Common Core State Standards (see appendix A, page 107) and possible look-for indicators of how the practices may actually occur in the classroom, with possible student and teacher behaviors noted. The look-fors provided in this table are merely examples and can be modified to seek particular student and teacher behaviors across or within the content domains of the CCSS. Such exemplars will help teachers and principals consider the importance of problem solving, reasoning, precision, modeling with mathematics, and instructional tools, as well as the importance of structure, regularity in reasoning, and communicating about the mathematics learned, as exhibited in the classroom. Consider use of the Mathematical Practices as a frame to organize student *and* teacher expectations when completing informal walkthroughs at your school site. Also consider using a grid similar to table 1.4, but without the suggested classroom indicators. You could then ask your teachers to fill in the blanks. What would they expect their students to do as they engage in the practices? What do they think they should be doing? Are there some practices that will be easier to access than others? Visit **go.solution-tree.com/leadership** for a blank, reproducible version of this table.

The practices represent the crucial first step in considering the content domains within the CCSS. The Mathematical Practices are thoroughly discussed as part of instruction in chapter 2.

Table 1.4: Mathematical Practices—Look-Fors as Classroom Indicators

Mathematical Practices	Look-Fors—Classroom Indicators
1. Make sense of problems and persevere in solving them.	Students: Are engaged in solving problems
	Teacher: Provides time for students to discuss problem solutions
2. Reason abstractly and quantitatively.	Students: Are able to contextualize and/or decontextualize problems
	Teacher: Provides access to and uses appropriate representations (manipulative materials, drawings, online renderings) of problems
3. Construct viable arguments and critique the reasoning of others.	Students: Understand and use prior learning in constructing arguments
	Teacher: Provides opportunities for students to listen to or read the conclusions and arguments of others
4. Model with mathematics.	Students: Analyze and model relationships mathematically (using an expression or equation)
	Teacher: Provides contexts for students to apply the mathematics learned
5. Use appropriate tools strategically.	Students: Have access to and use instructional tools to deepen understanding (manipulative materials, drawing, technological tools)
	Teacher: Uses appropriate tools (manipulatives) instructionally
6. Attend to precision.	Students: Recognize the need for precision in response to a problem; use appropriate mathematics vocabulary
	Teacher: Emphasizes the importance of precise communication, including appropriate use of mathematical vocabulary; emphasize the importance of accuracy and efficiency in solutions to problems, including use of estimation and mental mathematics, where appropriate
7. Look for and make use of structure.	Students: Should be encouraged to look for patterns and structure (use of properties; compose and decompose numbers) within mathematics
	Teacher: Provides time for students to discuss patterns that emerge in a problem's solution
8. Look for and express regularity in repeated reasoning.	Students: Reason about varied strategies and methods for solving problems; check for the reasonableness of their results
	Teacher: Encourages students to look for and discuss regularity in their reasoning

Source: Fennell, 2011b.

Content Alignment

The principal's vision for the daily expectations of mathematics content decisions should match the selection and use of instructional tools. In order to determine this alignment, it is necessary for principals to address the following with teacher teams:

- Does your mathematics curriculum embody and emphasize the CCSS student Mathematical Practices? Do the materials you select or use include activities that will engage students in the Mathematical Practices? If so, how?

- Does your school's mathematics curriculum emphasize content domains and standards that align with the standards and domains of the CCSS?

- Does your mathematics curriculum account for all the mathematical domains and standards of the CCSS in the materials you are selecting or currently using? Are the suggested activities appropriate, particularly as they involve the representation of key concepts and understandings?

- How important is problem solving in mathematics teaching and learning at your school? Do your mathematics curriculum materials align with the NCTM process standard for problem solving and the CCSS Mathematical Practice standard of "make sense of problems and persevere in solving them" and the related reasoning practices?

- Does your mathematics curriculum require your teachers to place an emphasis on conceptual understanding *and* procedural fluency? Do the curriculum materials you are using provide lessons and additional activities that address the Common Core State Standards—emphasizing conceptual understanding and fluency? How do you know? Is the balance consistent with your expectations?

The following feature box provides an example of what to look for relative to the Mathematical Practice "reason abstractly and quantitatively." What must occur before you can expect this practice to become part of the student classroom experience? To answer, consider students engaging in the following problem.

Reasoning Expectations

Cooper had 7 cards of a set of 38 cards. His brother and sister had the rest of the cards, with his brother Cameron having one more card than his sister Mia. How many cards did they each have?

If you think about the CCSS Mathematical Practice "reason abstractly and quantitatively," consider what you would like students to do here. What kinds of responses would you like to hear regarding their reasoning? How about the following?

    a. Well, 7 + some number is 38, so I counted up . . . 8, 9, 10 is 3, then 28 more, so 31 cards for the other two. Hmm. 15 + 16 is 31, so Cameron has 16 and Mia 15.

    b. OK, I subtracted 38 − 7 = 31; that's how much the brother and sister had. Half of 30 is 15 and one more is 16, so 7 + 15 + 16 = 38.

    c. I could think 7 + x + x + 1 = 38, since x + 1 is the one more card for Cameron. That would be 2x + 1 + 7 = 38 or 2x + 8 = 38; 2x = 38 − 8; 2x = 30; x = 30/2; x = 15; so 7 + 15 + 16 = 38.

Consider whether each response represents student reasoning and whether some solutions are more abstract than others.

Looking for evidence of reasoning can help you articulate the level of student understanding for these three different student responses, while determining whether they each include abstract and quantitative reasoning. You can then help teachers plan classroom activities and provide problems that engage their students in reasoning and in establishing a classroom climate that promotes and challenges student thinking and accepts a variety of solutions. The issue of importance here is engaging learners, all learners, in mathematical tasks that challenge and promote reasoning.

Priorities for Charting Improvement in Mathematics Content

The charge of the National Mathematics Advisory Panel (NMAP) was to "examine the critical skills and skill progressions for students to acquire competence in algebra" (2008, p. 7). The panel identified Critical Foundations of Algebra, which are prerequisite concepts and skills essentials for students prior to formal coursework in algebra. The Critical Foundations include the following:

1. Fluency with whole numbers

2. Fluency with fractions

3. Particular aspects of geometry and measurement

The NMAP's Critical Foundations, along with the Curriculum Focal Points (NCTM, 2006), helped frame the content domains of the CCSS. Note that fluency with whole numbers and fractions, and emphasis on particular aspects of geometry and measurement (such as perimeter and area), are bedrock topics and standards within the elementary school curriculum. Your responsibility is to ensure proficiency for these major topic essentials within the domains of the CCSS.

Teachers will need considerable support in aligning the mathematics they teach—their content—with the CCSS. They will also need opportunities to meet in cross-grade teams to discuss the content domain progressions. These meetings should aim to more specifically discuss and plan how teachers will address these progressions, which include experiences ranging from initial exposure to proficiency, across particular grades. The school's mathematics specialist or instructional leader should assist in supporting a school's grade-level team's progress in addressing these content issues.

The CCSS mathematics content, the domains and the related expectations within the CCSS, are the "what" of mathematics instruction; it's the math. The next chapter addresses the incredibly important "how to" issue—how to effectively design mathematics instruction that fosters student successful learning of the "what."

TWO

HIGH-QUALITY MATHEMATICS INSTRUCTION

High-quality mathematics curriculum and instructional materials consistent with the Common Core State Standards are indeed important. How teachers implement the curriculum, however, determines what students will actually learn. Understanding the nature of high-quality mathematics instruction, and what teachers and students should be doing in the classroom, is essential for your role as instructional leader of your school. Such understanding is the basis for monitoring and evaluating instruction, assessing what teachers need to improve their instruction, and designing and supporting appropriate professional development. The Mathematical Practices (CCSSO, 2010a) and classroom indicators from chapter 1 provide an initial vision of what both students and teachers should be doing as part of the learning process.

This chapter first characterizes mathematics teaching and considers research about how students learn mathematics, then describes eight essential instructional practices that research supports as most effective in helping students become mathematically proficient, such as understand mathematical ideas, acquire skills, and develop fluency in the CCSS Mathematical Practices.

Research That Informs Instruction

Mathematics teaching can be defined as the "product of the interactions among the teacher, the students, and the mathematics in an instructional triangle" (NRC, 2001, p. 313). Figure 2.1 (page 22) illustrates this view.

While the teachers' knowledge, decisions, and actions are a central aspect of teaching, they are not the only factors that determine what is taught and learned. Figure 2.1 highlights a second component centered on student actions and learning experiences: how students engage with the instructional materials and teacher actions, and how they use the background

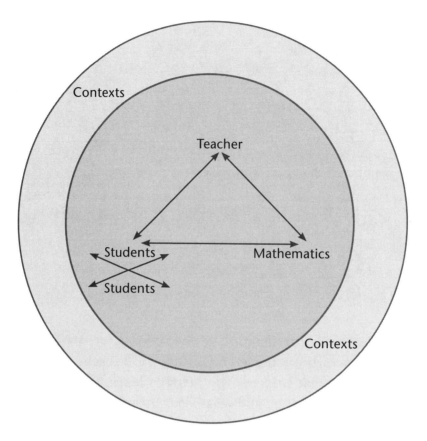

Source: NRC, 2001, p. 314. Used with permission.

Figure 2.1: The instructional triangle shows instruction as the interaction among teachers, students, and mathematics in contexts.

knowledge and beliefs they bring to learning. Student interactions with other students also play a crucial role in what is learned.

The third instructional component is the mathematics content, which refers to the mathematical ideas, concepts, and skills to be learned, as well as how the content is represented in the instructional tasks and curriculum materials used in the classroom. The interactions among all three of these components are what ultimately produce student learning.

As figure 2.1 shows, the interactions among teachers, students, and content occur in contexts. *Contexts* refers to the wide range of factors that influence instruction, including district and school policies, school organization, school leadership, and external assessments and related policies. Thus when characterizing mathematics instruction within your school, you must consider the influence of these contextual factors on the teacher-students-content interactions and your role as principal in creating or mitigating these factors.

Research from both cognitive science (Bransford, Brown, & Cocking, 2000) and mathematics education (Bransford & Donovan, 2005; Donovan & Bransford, 2005; Hiebert & Grouws, 2007) supports the characterization of mathematics learning as an active process in which students build their own mathematical knowledge from experience in conjunction with feedback from peers, teachers and other adults, and themselves. In addition, this research has identified a number of core principles of learning that are particularly important for teachers to understand and incorporate into their instruction. Specifically, learners should:

- Engage with challenging tasks that involve active meaning making

- Connect new learning with prior knowledge, and in the process, address preconceptions and misconceptions

- Acquire conceptual knowledge and skills to enable them to organize their knowledge, transfer knowledge to new situations, and acquire new knowledge

- Socially construct knowledge through talk, activity, and interaction around meaningful problems

- Receive timely feedback so they can revise their work, thinking, and understandings

- Develop metacognitive awareness of themselves as learners, thinkers, and problem solvers, and learn to monitor their learning and performance

These essential learning principles provide the research basis for the following eight strategies of effective mathematics instruction.

Visit **go.solution-tree.com/leadership** for further resources regarding instruction.

Instructional Strategies and the CCSS Mathematical Practices

Research on mathematics teaching, along with the learning principles described previously, has identified eight key instructional strategies that produce increased student learning (Bransford & Donovan, 2005; Dweck, 2007; Franke, Kazemi, & Battery, 2007; Fuson, Kalchman, & Bransford, 2005; Henningson & Stein, 1997; Hiebert & Grouws, 2007; NRC, 2001; Pashler et al., 2007; Resnick, 2006; Swan, 2005; Wiliam, 2007a, 2007b). Table 2.1 lists these strategies and highlights how their support for mathematics learning is explicitly connected to the CCSS Mathematical Practices (listed in appendix A, page 107). These strategies are *meta-strategies*—instructional practices that should be incorporated into lessons on a regular basis, regardless of the specific mathematics concepts or skills being taught. As such, these are important look-fors as you observe classrooms and discuss instruction with the teachers in your school.

Table 2.1: Instructional Strategies That Promote Student Achievement

Instructional Strategy	Mathematical Practices
1. Active engagement	*Incorporate as an essential element for every CCSS Mathematical Practice.*
2. Solving challenging problems	Make sense of problems and persevere in solving them. Construct viable arguments and critique the reasoning of others.
3. Connecting ideas, concepts, and skills	Make sense of problems and persevere in solving them. Reason abstractly and quantitatively. Construct viable arguments and critique the reasoning of others. Model with mathematics. Look for and make use of structure. Look for and express regularity in repeated reasoning.
4. Communicating mathematically	Make sense of problems and persevere in solving them. Construct viable arguments and critique the reasoning of others. Attend to precision.
5. Engaging students' prior knowledge	Make sense of problems and persevere in solving them. Construct viable arguments and critique the reasoning of others. Look for and make use of structure. Look for and express regularity in repeated reasoning.
6. Using ongoing, distributed practice with appropriate feedback	*Incorporate as an essential element for every CCSS Mathematical Practice.*
7. Using appropriate tools strategically	Use appropriate tools strategically.
8. Promoting students' positive self-beliefs	Make sense of problems and persevere in solving them.

*Visit **go.solution-tree.com/leadership** for a reproducible version of this table.*

Active Engagement

Students should be "doing the math"—solving problems, analyzing solutions, explaining mathematical ideas—not simply watching the teacher or other students solve problems, answer questions, or explain ideas and procedures.

To illustrate the difference, Wood (2001) provides the following two short interchanges between a teacher and her grade 2 students.

> Tchr: [The teacher has made 45 tally marks on the board and has circled 4 groups of ten.] We have 4 groups of ten, and how many left over?
>
> Beth: 4 tens
>
> Sara: 5
>
> Tchr: 5. Now can anybody tell me what number that could be? We have 4 tens and 5 ones. What is that number, Ann?

Ann: [remains silent]

Tchr: If we have 4 tens and 5 ones, what is that number?

Ann: 9

Tchr: Look at how many we have there [points to the 4 groups of ten] and 5 ones. If we have 4 tens and 5 ones, we have—? [voice rises] 45.

Class: 45

Tchr: Very good. (p. 110)

In the next interchange, the children have just discussed how they solved the problem $39 + 24 = 63$, and they are now discussing how to find the sum of $39 + 25 = \underline{\hspace{1.5cm}}$.

Tchr: Now, the next one, 39 plus 25, John and Dan.

John: We got 64.

Tchr: Explain how you got this answer.

John: Well, we know that 39 plus 20 is 59. And then 5 more would make it 64.

Tchr: All right. Let's hear from Anna and Carol. How did you solve this problem?

Anna: I did it a different way than John said. You can also go like I . . . [she goes to the board] these two are the same [points to the 39 in each problem]. But 24 to 25 is just one higher, so 64. (p. 110)

In the second exchange, students explain *their* ways of finding the sum of 39 and 25, in contrast to the first exchange, in which the teacher provides the mathematical ideas, while some students answer isolated questions. A key question to determine the quality of mathematics instruction, then, is, Who is doing the mathematical thinking?

Letting students actively do the math is a vital instructional behavior in order to develop students' conceptual understanding and proficiency in the CCSS Mathematical Practices. These practices, detailed in appendix A (page 107), describe what this *doing* should look like in the classroom (for example, solving problems, constructing viable arguments, critiquing the reasoning of others, creating mathematical models, and using tools strategically).

Solving Challenging Problems

According to Lappan and Briars (1995), "there is no decision that teachers make that has a greater impact on students' opportunities to learn and on their perceptions about what mathematics is than the selection or creation of the tasks with which the teacher engages students in studying mathematics" (p. 139).

The term *mathematical tasks* refers to a single complex problem or a set of problems used to focus students' attention on a particular mathematical idea (Smith & Stein, 1998). Tasks are important because they form the basis for students to learn what mathematics is and how one does it. Tasks influence what students learn by directing their attention to specific aspects of content and by detailing ways to process information. Most important, the level and kind of thinking that instructional tasks require, referred to as the *level of cognitive demand*, influences what students learn (Henningson & Stein, 1997). Table 2.2 shows examples of tasks with different levels of cognitive demand.

Table 2.2: Lower- and Higher-Level Cognitive Demand Tasks

Lower-Level Demand	Higher-Level Demand
Memorization What are the decimal equivalents for the fractions ½ and ¼? What is the place value of the underlined digits: 10<u>3</u> <u>2</u>,011 19.<u>8</u>	*Procedures with connections* Using a 10 x 10 grid, identify the decimal and percent equivalents of ⅗. Solve this problem in two different ways: *Michael had 82¢. He spent 49¢ on stickers. How much does he have left?* Explain what you were thinking as you solved it.
Procedures without connections Rewrite ⅜ as a decimal. 22 x 11 = Frank wants to carpet his bedroom, which is 9 feet wide and 12 feet long. How many square feet of carpeting does he need?	*Doing mathematics* Tracey is making dot patterns Pattern 1 Pattern 2 Pattern 3 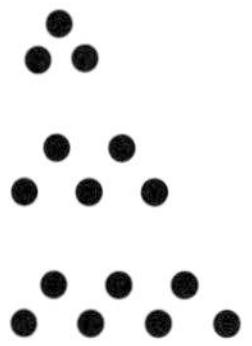 1. Draw dot patterns 4 and 5. 2. Figure out how many dots will be in pattern 10 without drawing it. ⅗ is more than 3/7. Explain how you know this is true. José ate ½ of a pizza. Ella ate ½ of another pizza. José said that he ate more pizza than Ella, but Ella said they both ate the same amount. Use words and pictures to show that José could be right (NAEP, 1992).

To clarify further, level of cognitive demand refers to the type of thinking that tasks require of students. Cognitive demand is different from the following:

- *Difficulty*—Some tasks may be more difficult for students than others, but that does not mean the tasks require different types of thinking. For example, both 69×78 and 22×11 are lower-level cognitive demand "procedures without connections" tasks, even though the first task is computationally more challenging than the second.

- *Importance*—It is important for students to be able to do certain lower-level cognitive demand tasks, such as the immediate recall of the decimal equivalents for the common fractions ½, ⅓, ¼, ¾, ⅕, or to know a procedure for finding the decimal equivalents for any fraction (procedures without connections). However, initially developing students' underlying conceptual understanding through engagement in higher-level cognitive demand tasks facilitates learning and retention of these lower-demand skills.

Engaging students in solving higher-level cognitive demand tasks on a regular basis is essential for students' acquisition of the CCSS Mathematical Practices, especially "make sense of problems" and "construct viable arguments." Making sense of problems includes building a toolkit of problem-solving strategies and developing perseverance (that is, recognizing some problems take longer than a few minutes to solve). Doing so requires students to have repeated opportunities to solve challenging problems. Furthermore, explaining and comparing problem solutions is a natural way to develop students' abilities to construct arguments and critique others' arguments.

Regular work on challenging problems also develops students' understanding of mathematics in general (Hiebert & Grouws, 2007). A growing body of research links students' engagement in higher-level cognitive demand tasks to overall increases in mathematics learning, not just in the ability to solve problems (Resnick, 2006).

It is the principal's role to ensure *all* teachers use higher-level cognitive demand tasks as an integral part of students' learning experiences during a unit of study. Steps include analyzing resources available to teachers, as well as instruction, such as the following:

1. *Examine your instructional materials*—Do the materials regularly include higher-level cognitive demand tasks as core learning activities for all students to support teachers' use of such tasks?

2. *Examine your assessments including classroom, district, and external summative assessments*—Do these assessments include higher-level tasks?

3. *Monitor instruction and examine the extent to which students are cognitively engaged*—How is the teacher ensuring that all students are engaged with the task and the mathematics they are to learn (Boaler & Humphreys, 2005; Wiliam, 2007b)?

While students are working on tasks, teachers should circulate, monitoring students' progress by asking advancing and assessing questions that help student progress in solving the task. Too often, teachers decrease the cognitive demand of a task by doing too much of the thinking for the students, either in setting up the task or in leading students step-by-step instead of letting students engage with the problem themselves (Weiss & Pasley, 2004).

To close lessons, teachers should engage students in summary or debriefing discussions around the important mathematical ideas explicit to understanding the lesson. In such discussions, the students, not the teacher, should do most of the talking. Stein, Engle, Smith, and Hughes (2008) identify five instructional practices (highlighted in the feature box on page 28) for orchestrating productive mathematics discussions as students work on challenging tasks.

Orchestrating Mathematical Discourse

1. Anticipate the array of strategies—both correct and incorrect—that students might use to solve a problem and how those strategies relate to the mathematical concepts, representations, procedures, and practices the teacher would like students to learn.

2. Monitor students' responses as they explore a task, making note of particular strategies, representations, and other ideas that would be important to share during a whole-class discussion.

3. Select specific students to share their work with the rest of the class in order to make particular mathematical ideas public.

4. Sequence student responses in a particular way so as to maximize the chances that the mathematical goals for the discussion will be achieved.

5. Connect different responses so that students can understand how the same mathematical idea is embedded in different strategies.

Source: Smith & Stein, 2011; Stein et al., 2008.

These five considerations for orchestrating discourse can be valuable foci for ongoing professional development, especially for grade-level teams. Joint team planning for how to best implement a particular task, followed by team reflection on task implementation (using audio or a videotape of the lesson or samples of student work), is a valuable strategy for continuous improvement of mathematics instruction.

Connecting Ideas, Concepts, and Skills

In addition to engaging students in solving challenging tasks, explicit attention must be given to connections among ideas, facts, and procedures that promote students' conceptual understanding (Hiebert & Grouws, 2007). Teachers help students make these connections when they:

- Challenge students to make sense of what they are doing to solve mathematics problems

- Pose questions that stimulate students' thinking, asking them to justify their conclusions, strategies, and procedures

- Have students evaluate and explain the work of other students, and compare and contrast different solution methods for the same problem

- Ask students to represent the same ideas in multiple ways (symbolically, pictorially, or with manipulatives)

As this list shows, connecting ideas, concepts, and skills is an inherent aspect of a number of the CCSS Mathematical Practices, especially "model with mathematics," which requires students to represent the same relationships in multiple ways. Students illustrate the practice of "reason abstractly and quantitatively" when they symbolically represent a problem situation and can move between its symbolic (abstract) and concrete representations. To develop this practice, students need explicit opportunities to both decontextualize ("Write a number sentence that describes a particular situation") and contextualize a situation ("Write a story problem that could be represented by ___ = 8 × 7"). Students develop the practices of "look for and make use of structure" and "look for and express regularity in repeated reasoning" when teachers engage them in looking for patterns and making connections across problems or calculations.

Pashler and colleagues (2007) indicate that explicitly illustrating links between ideas by describing specific connections among representations helps students make such associations. For example, when students write equations to represent situations ("Write 27 + ___ = 35"), it is helpful to ask them to explicitly show or describe what each of the numbers represents.

Communicating Mathematically

An integral part of the three previously described instructional strategies is for students to discuss, explain, and mathematically justify their reasoning.

Mathematics lessons should provide many opportunities for students to communicate their ideas rather than being limited to summary discussions. Communicating mathematically includes drawing pictures or diagrams to explain ideas, writing in mathematics journals, presenting problem-solution strategies to the class, and using chart paper, transparencies, or document cameras. As figure 2.1 (page 22) indicates, student-student talk, not just student-teacher talk, is an important communication expectation for teacher planning and is a look-for as you visit classrooms.

Student-student communication is exactly what is expected in the CCSS Mathematical Practices "construct viable arguments and critique the reasoning of others" and "make sense of problems." These practices require communication. Simply solving a problem and checking if the answer is correct is not enough; these practices explicitly require students to explain their solutions and compare and contrast one's own solution to classmates' solutions.

Communicating mathematically requires more than students talking to each other. The quality of students' communication—in particular, precise use of vocabulary and symbols as described in the Mathematical Practice "attend to precision"—is a critical area to identify in mathematics classes. Grade-level teachers should explicitly help students recognize the difference between mathematical terms and everyday use of the same word. For instance, in everyday language, *diagonal* refers to a slanted line; in mathematics, a *diagonal* of a polygon can be a horizontal or vertical line segment, as well as a slanted one. Teachers should also model correct use of symbols, especially the equal sign. For example, consider the following vignette:

> Third graders are trying to figure out how to use 8, 7, 3, 9, and 2 to make 8. One student offers this solution, "Add 8 and 9 to get 17, then subtract 7 to get 10, then divide by 2 to get 5, then add 3 to get 8." The teacher records these steps as follows:
>
> $$8 + 9 = 17 - 7 = 10 \div 2 = 5 + 3 = 8$$

What's wrong? Step back and read the entire equation. It says $8 + 9 = 8$!

Using = as a universal connector is a common bad habit of teachers as well as students. Instead, each step should be written as a separate (true) equation.

Teachers support students' attention to precision when they model careful use of language and symbols and encourage students to do the same, as illustrated in the equal-sign example. While it is not essential that young children use formal names for mathematical properties (such as *commutative* or *associative property*), students should be encouraged to use precise terms that are accessible, such as *numerator* and *denominator* instead of *top number* and *bottom number*, *sum* and *difference* instead of *answer*, and so on.

Providing students occasions to regularly work with a partner maximizes communication opportunities. In partner work, each child has a clear right and responsibility to communicate with the partner—and does not have the option to sit back and let others do the talking and thinking, which sometimes happens during group work. Many teachers find it effective to organize students in pairs; then they combine pairs when they want small-group teamwork.

Engaging Students' Prior Knowledge

Bransford and colleagues (2000) highlight a predominant view of student learning that illustrates how students build new knowledge based on what they already know and believe. Thus an individual's prior knowledge significantly influences what is learned in a particular situation. Effective instruction explicitly helps learners connect new ideas with what they already know and understand. In mathematics instruction, there are three different aspects to connecting students' prior knowledge: (1) building new learning on students' existing mathematical knowledge, including their informal mathematical knowledge; (2) engaging students' preconceptions about mathematics, especially those that may interfere with mathematics learning; and (3) addressing students' misconceptions.

Building New Learning on Students' Existing Mathematical Knowledge

Students enter school with considerable knowledge about their world, including informal strategies for solving problems. For example, most kindergarteners can solve straightforward addition and subtraction situation problems prior to formal instruction (for example, Emily has 5 pennies. She finds 3 more. How many pennies does she have now?). They achieve this by simply acting out the problems, using their counting knowledge and knowledge about "getting more" and "taking away." More important, researchers have found that engaging students in solving such problems before introducing formal addition and subtraction vocabulary and symbols facilitates students' understanding of these operations (Cross et al., 2009; NRC, 2001). In other words, the formal mathematical operations make more sense to students when they can relate them to situations they already understand—like getting more and taking away.

Engaging students' informal knowledge at the onset of instruction is valuable and applies to other mathematical concepts as well. For example, first and second graders are able to use their knowledge of counting, sharing, adding, and subtracting to solve simple multiplication and division word problems, such as:

- There are 4 bags with 3 cookies in each bag. How many cookies are there in all?

- If 4 children share 12 cookies equally, how many cookies will each child get?

This provides a basis for formal instruction in these latter operations in grades 3 and 4. Similarly, the Institute of Education Sciences practice guide, *Developing Effective Fractions Instruction for Kindergarten Through 8th Grade* (Siegler et al., 2010), recommends that initial fraction instruction be built on students' informal understanding of sharing. That is, the concept of fractions should be introduced through equal-sharing activities that involve both dividing sets of objects as well as single whole objects. Introducing fractions as equal shares is precisely the approach to fraction development called for in CCSS in grades 1 and 2 (CCSSO, 2010a).

The use of informal knowledge as a starting point for instruction applies to learning computation procedures as well. Students can use their conceptual knowledge of counting, operations and their properties, and place value to create their own strategies for solving multi-digit addition, subtraction, multiplication, and division problems before being taught standard algorithms. This type of progression—from conceptual knowledge, to informal conceptually based strategies, to a formal algorithm—is precisely the progression that CCSS describes for the development of computational fluency.

Engaging Students' Preconceptions About Mathematics

In addition to informal knowledge and reasoning, children may also have preconceptions about mathematics (Fuson et al., 2005). Three common preconceptions can interfere with mathematics learning if not addressed:

1. Mathematics is about learning to compute.

2. Mathematics is about following rules to guarantee correct answers.

3. Some people have the ability to do math and some don't.

Instead, students should understand that mathematics is about solving important and relevant problems, that standard procedures are clever inventions that help one solve complex problems more easily, and that everyone can be successful in mathematics with hard work and effort. The latter is an important component of developing the perseverance and disposition aspects of the Mathematical Practice "make sense of problems." Unfortunately, these preconceptions are often a result of students' early school experiences. The next challenge, then, is to prevent students from forming these erroneous preconceptions, or to dispel them if they already exist. Fuson et al. (2005) identify several features of instruction that address these preconceptions:

- Allow and encourage students to use their own informal strategies before introducing more standard strategies and procedures.

- Provide opportunities for students to describe and discuss their strategies, why they work, and compare and contrast different strategies.

- Design instructional activities to connect students' ideas to the mathematical understandings they are to develop. (p. 223)

Mark says ¼ of his candy bar is smaller than ⅕ of the same candy bar. He drew this picture to explain his answer.

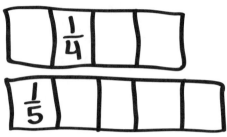

Mark's answer is wrong. Use pictures and words to explain why Mark's answer is not correct.

Source: Adapted from NAEP, 2007.

Figure 2.2: Addressing misconceptions.

Addressing Students' Misconceptions

Sometimes, the prior knowledge that students have about a mathematical idea is flawed; that is, they have misconceptions. Misconceptions may be overgeneralizations of correct mathematics ideas, such as applying ideas about whole numbers to fractions and decimals (for instance, $\frac{1}{2} < \frac{1}{4}$ because $2 < 4$; $0.23 > 0.7$ because $23 > 7$; or in multiplication, the product is always greater than either of the two factors, which is true for whole numbers but not fractions and decimals). (See fig. 2.2 for an example.) When teachers attempt to build new learning on prior knowledge, it is important to expose and address misconceptions students may have.

Asking students to analyze and explain examples of both correct and incorrect solutions that anticipate common student misconceptions pushes students to more deeply process and reason with greater understanding, and thus can prevent them from forming misconceptions in the first place. It also helps students develop the Mathematical Practice "construct viable arguments and critique the reasoning of others."

Strategies for repairing "flawed prior knowledge" have important implications for the design of interventions for struggling students. Too often, educators treat such students as if they have no knowledge of previously taught concepts and skills. In most cases, however, struggling students do have prior knowledge of the content in question—the problem is, that knowledge is flawed. Successful interventions engage students in tasks that expose their misconceptions and help them analyze why their ideas are flawed. Activities such as working with a partner to analyze worked examples prove to be more effective than the typical remediation approach of reteaching (Swan, 2005).

Students' incorrect preconceptions and misconceptions are often the result of teacher (and parent) behaviors. While not intentional, particular instructional practices can promote misconceptions, either explicitly or implicitly. Teachers need to be aware of these practices and their potential *negative* effect on students' learning. A few common examples include:

- *Teaching students the steps in a computational procedure without providing opportunities for students to first develop their own informal strategies or without letting students learn and discuss the mathematical reasons for the steps*—A prevalent example of this is teaching the long division algorithm by emphasizing the sequence of steps (divide, multiply, subtract, check, bring down), sometimes even with a mnemonic to help students remember the steps (such as **D**oes **M**cDonald's **S**ell **C**heese **B**urgers), without developing an understanding of why this algorithm works.

- *Using limited examples that distort or narrow students' understanding of a concept*—For example, always drawing equilateral or nearly equilateral triangles (△) can lead students to think that "less" equilateral-looking triangles are not triangles at all. Similarly, always writing number sentences in a particular form, such as $15 + 7 = 22$, instead of using other forms, such as $22 = 15 + 7$; $22 = 22$; and $15 + 7 = 14 + 8$, can lead students to think that $=$ means "the answer is next" instead of as a symbol that denotes equal quantities.

- *Giving incorrect mathematical information that has to be undone later*—For example, telling students that they can't subtract 10 from 8 will be confusing later, when they learn negative numbers.

- *Giving students procedures for solving problems that only work in a limited number of cases*—For example, teaching students to use key words to solve word problems (*left* or *left over* tells you to subtract; "How many in all?" tells you to add, and so on) instead of teaching children to think about the part/whole relationships among the quantities in the problem.

Teaching mnemonics for the division algorithm and the key words strategy are examples of "teaching for answers" rather than "teaching for mathematical understanding." This is an important distinction for the principal and the grade-level teams to consider during lesson planning and observations. Teaching for understanding naturally engages students in the Mathematical Practices of looking for and making use of structure, constructing viable arguments, making sense of problems, and looking for and expressing regularity in repeated reasoning.

Using Ongoing, Distributed Practice With Appropriate Feedback

One of the better established, yet underapplied, results from research on effective instruction is that periodic opportunities to practice concepts and skills, along with feedback about performance, improve student learning and retention (Pashler et al., 2007). Distributed practice with feedback helps students solidify their knowledge and promotes retention, reflection, generalization, and transfer of knowledge and skill. In other words, smaller numbers of practice problems, given regularly with feedback about correctness, better support student learning and retention of mathematics content than massed practice—especially massed practice immediately after a concept or skill has been introduced.

Distributed practice can be achieved using a variety of methods—daily warm-ups, for instance, or review problems as part of homework, quizzes, or classroom questions. Regardless of the method, it is important to create periodic classroom opportunities for students to recall and apply concepts and skills, with feedback about their work. This practice should include concepts and skills from previous courses and grades, not just those taught in the current mathematics class.

The research about distributed practice has particularly important implications for a pervasive school assessment practice such as *test prep* (placing regular instruction on hold in order to prepare for state assessments). While on the surface this may appear to make sense, studies indicate just the opposite—test scores are actually lower in schools that spend large amounts of time on test prep (Allensworth, Correa, & Ponisciak, 2008). Instead, to prepare for state assessments, teachers should regularly engage students in tasks that review, practice, and use previously taught concepts and skills throughout the school year.

As principal, one of the most important steps for increasing student learning is to provide time for teachers to develop a plan for ongoing, distributed practice that they can incorporate into their daily instruction.

Using Appropriate Tools Strategically

The strategic use of appropriate tools is, in fact, one of the CCSS Mathematical Practices. Manipulatives, student drawings, electronic interactive boards, calculators, computers, and other devices can be powerful instructional tools that support student learning of mathematics. The use of such tools is a means to an end for mathematics learning—not an end in itself. The quality of mathematics instruction depends on *how* students are using these tools to help make sense of the mathematics and to solve problems. The mere presence or use of such tools is not an indicator of the quality of the instruction.

Manipulatives best support mathematics learning when students are prompted to explicitly relate them to the mathematical ideas to be learned. For example, when students use base-ten materials to model how they solved a multidigit subtraction problem, they should explicitly connect how they used the blocks to their symbolic representation of the solution process. In addition to physical materials, a wide variety of virtual manipulatives are now available free on the Internet and can be found at the National Library of Virtual Manipulatives (http://matti.usu.edu/nlvm/nav/vlibrary.html) or in the electronic examples at the NCTM website (http://nctm.org). Computer software programs specifically designed to support children's development of problem solving or to develop automaticity with computational skills are also available. As principal, you have two important considerations if you're involved with software-purchasing decisions: (1) the type of mathematics thinking students are doing when using the software and (2) how this software contributes to students' mathematics learning.

Calculators are also effective instructional tools for two reasons. First, they enable children to tackle interesting real-world problems with "messy numbers" that exceed children's computational capabilities. Second, calculators can help students learn new mathematics by supporting explorations of patterns across repeated calculations (thus developing the Mathematical Practice "look for and express regularities in repeated reasoning"). Research findings across a large number of studies indicated that appropriate calculator use does not decrease students' computational skills (Hembree & Dessart, 1986). Regardless of calculator use, children still need to develop basic computational fluency without a calculator. They need to learn basic facts, computational procedures with reasonably sized numbers, and estimation techniques.

When tedious computations are involved, most adults use estimation or calculators, and children should learn when and how to use these strategies, too. This is precisely the intent of the CCSS Mathematical Practice "use appropriate tools strategically." Students not only need a variety of tools available, but they also need sufficient experience with a variety of tools and to be engaged in tasks that help them learn to make sound choices about when to use a particular tool. The flowchart in figure 2.3 illustrates how proficient students might select an appropriate computational tool or approach for a given problem.

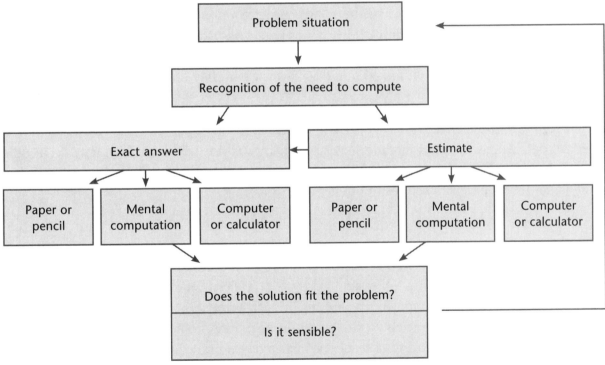

Figure 2.3: Computational model for mathematics problems and tasks.

Promoting Students' Positive Self-Beliefs

Students' perceptions of themselves as learners are important factors in their success in learning mathematics. Such perceptions are implicit in all of the Mathematical Practices and are explicitly referenced in the Mathematical Practice "make sense of problems and persevere in solving them." Mathematically proficient students view mathematics as "sensible, useful and worthwhile" (CCSSO, 2010a, p. 6) and believe that their success is a function of hard work and diligence.

Carol Dweck (2007) presents long-term research regarding students' beliefs about themselves as learners and how that affects academic behavior. Dweck indicates that students' beliefs about their intelligence—whether intelligence is a fixed trait (fixed mindset) or one that can grow over time (growth mindset)—is at the core of optimal math motivation and directly influences students' motivation to learn mathematics. Specifically, students with fixed mindsets care most about whether they will be judged as smart or not, so they reject learning opportunities if they might make mistakes, try to hide mistakes or deficiencies rather than correct them, are afraid of effort because it makes them feel dumb, and decrease their efforts when they hit a setback because they do not see any way to improve.

In contrast, students with growth mindsets care most about learning. They work to correct mistakes or deficiencies, view effort as positive, and escalate efforts when confronted with setbacks. When facing challenging school transitions or courses, students with growth mindsets outperform those with fixed mindsets, even when they entered with equal skills and knowledge (Dweck, 2007).

Fortunately, students can develop growth mindsets through instruction. Dweck has developed an online instructional module (www.brainology.us) for upper elementary and middle school students that explicitly teaches students about the brain and its functions and that intellectual development is the result of effort and learning.

The type of praise teachers provide is central to this issue. When teachers use praise that refers to students' intelligence ("Excellent work, Tim. You are so smart."), they foster fixed mindsets. In contrast, praise that explicitly refers to effort, engagement, perseverance, and so forth ("Excellent work, Tim. I can see that you put a lot of time and effort into your work on that problem. It really paid off.") promotes growth mindsets (Mueller & Dweck, 1998). Providing feedback to teachers about the type of praise they provide is an important component of the principal's monitoring of teachers' instructional practices.

Priorities for Charting Improvement in Mathematics Instruction

Thoughtful planning is essential for teachers to enact lessons that promote both the content and practices aspirations of CCSS. Smith, Bill, and Hughes (2008) have created the "thinking through a lesson protocol" (TTLP)—a process to help teachers collaboratively plan lessons that implement high-level tasks. The protocol provides specific questions that help teachers explicitly plan how they will select and set up tasks, support students' exploration of the task, and orchestrate the sharing and closing discussion.

The TTLP is also a useful tool for principals in that it highlights instruction features to look for in classroom observations and provides discussion questions for pre- and postobservation conferences. It is important to remember that TTLP is intended for collaborative grade-level planning around high-level tasks during a unit of instruction, and not for every daily lesson design. TTLP, for instance, could be used to advance a lesson study project for a teacher grade-level team. Ultimately, working with the TTLP should provide teachers with a set of questions to guide their instructional planning. Figure 2.4 (page 38) provides the TTLP and table 2.3 (page 39) provides a template for using the TTLP.

While good classroom management and effective classroom routines help teachers establish classrooms as learning communities, they are just the first steps. In addition, teachers need to both develop classroom norms about what it means to "do mathematics" and build relationships with and among students to support mathematics learning (Franke et al. 2007).

For example, Franke and Carey (1996) found that first graders had already figured out what it meant to succeed at mathematics in their classroom: you had to be fast at it, and if the teacher asked you a question about your answer, it was wrong. Replacing these conceptions with an expectation for students to always explain an answer whether it's right or wrong, or that it can take longer than a few seconds to solve a problem, are essential ways to establish a classroom learning community that truly focuses on the Mathematical Practice "make sense of problems and persevere in solving them."

In learning community classrooms, teachers encourage children to develop divergent solutions and inventive ideas that are presented to the whole group. Children listen to and talk with each other, show respect for one another's ideas, even when they disagree, and use each other as resources for solving mathematical problems.

As the instructional leader of the school, one of your major responsibilities is to ensure *every* teacher in the school provides high-quality mathematics instruction based on the strategies described in this chapter. Just as you expect teachers to set high expectations and address the learning needs of every student in their classes; it is your responsibility to address the learning needs of every teacher in the school and support them so they can implement high-quality mathematics instruction in their classrooms daily. You must ask if all students in your school engage in high-quality mathematics instruction about important, meaningful mathematics every day.

The true measure of instructional quality is the mathematics that students learn from it. Thus assessing student learning is an integral part of high-quality instruction. The next chapter examines the features of high-quality assessment and introduces a five-step assessment cycle for continuous improvement of learning and instruction.

PART 1: SELECTING AND SETTING UP A MATHEMATICAL TASK

What are your mathematical goals for the lesson (i.e., what do you want students to know and understand about mathematics as a result of this lesson)?

In what ways does the task build on students' previous knowledge, life experiences, and culture? What definitions, concepts, or ideas do students need to know to begin to work on the task? What questions will you ask to help students access their prior knowledge and relevant life and cultural experiences?

What are all the ways the task can be solved?

- Which of these methods do you think your students will use?
- What misconceptions might students have?
- What errors might students make?

What particular challenges might the task present to struggling students or students who are English Language Learners (ELL)? How will you address these challenges?

What are your expectations for students as they work on and complete this task?

- What resources or tools will students have to use in their work that will give them entry into, and help them reason through, the task?
- How will students work—independently, in small groups, or in pairs—to explore this task? How long will they work individually or in small groups or pairs? Will students be partnered in a specific way? If so, in what way?
- How will students record and report their work?

How will you introduce students to the activity so as to provide access to *all* students while maintaining the cognitive demands of the task? How will you ensure that students understand the context of the problem? What will you hear that lets you know students understand what the task is asking them to do?

PART 2: SUPPORTING STUDENTS' EXPLORATION OF THE TASK

As students work independently or in small groups, what questions will you ask to—

- Help a group get started or make progress on the task?
- Focus students' thinking on the key mathematical ideas in the task?
- Assess students' understanding of key mathematical ideas, problem-solving strategies, or the representations?

- Advance students' understanding of the mathematical ideas?
- Encourage all students to share their thinking with others or to assess their understanding of their peers' ideas?

How will you ensure that students remain engaged in the task?

- What assistance will you give or what questions will you ask a student (or group) who becomes quickly frustrated and requests more direction and guidance in solving the task?
- What will you do if a student (or group) finishes the task almost immediately? How will you extend the task so as to provide additional challenge?
- What will you do if a student (or group) focuses on nonmathematical aspects of the activity (e.g., spends most of his or her (or their) time making a poster of their work)?

PART 3: SHARING AND DISCUSSING THE TASK

How will you orchestrate the class discussion so that you accomplish your mathematical goals?

- Which solution paths do you want to have shared during the class discussion? In what order will the solutions be presented? Why?
- In what ways will the order in which solutions are presented help develop students' understanding of the mathematical ideas that are the focus of your lesson?
- What specific questions will you ask so that students will—
    1. Make sense of the mathematical ideas that you want them to learn?
    2. Expand on, debate, and question the solutions being shared?
    3. Make connections among the different strategies that are presented?
    4. Look for patterns?
    5. Begin to form generalizations?

How will you ensure that, over time, *each* student has the opportunity to share his or her thinking and reasoning with their peers?

What will you see or hear that lets you know that *all* students in the class understand the mathematical ideas that you intended for them to learn?

What will you do tomorrow that will build on this lesson?

Figure 2.4: Thinking through a lesson protocol.

Table 2.3: Thinking Through a Lesson Protocol Planning Template

Part 1: Selecting and Setting Up a Mathematical Task	
Learning Goal/Standard *What understandings will students take away from this lesson?*	**Evidence** *What will students say, do, produce, and so forth that will provide evidence of their understandings?*
Task/Activity What is the main activity that students will be working on in this lesson?	**Instructional Support—Tools, Resources** What tools or resources will students have to use in their work that will give them entry to, and help them reason through, the activity?
Task Enactment What are the various ways that students might complete the activity?	**Instructional Support—Teacher** What questions might you ask students that will support their exploration of the activity and provide a bridge between what they did and what they are expected to learn?

Part 2: Supporting Students' Exploration of the Task
What questions will you ask to help a pair or group get started? How will you focus students' thinking on the key mathematical ideas?
To be clear on what students actually did, begin by asking a set of assessing questions such as: What did you do? How did you get that? What does this mean? Once you have a clearer sense of what the student understands, move on to questions specific to the task/activity.
How will you ensure that students remain engaged in the task?
How will you assist a student/pair/group who become frustrated?
What will you ask "early finishers" to do?

continued →

Part 3: Sharing and Discussing the Task	
Selecting and Sequencing Which solutions do you want to have shared during the lesson? In what order? Why?	**Connecting Responses** What specific questions will you ask so that students make sense of the mathematical ideas they are expected to learn and make connections among the different strategies or solutions presented?

Source: Adapted from Smith et al., 2008. Visit **go.solution-tree.com/leadership** *for a reproducible version of this table.*

THREE
HIGH-QUALITY MATHEMATICS ASSESSMENT

Assessment gathers information about student learning and teacher practice to inform your daily decision making, adjust your administrative expectations for instruction and lesson design, and help your grade-level teacher teams revise teaching learning targets as needed. You understand, then, that effective assessment is no longer an isolated teacher act; it is grounded in the ongoing retrieval and analysis of information regarding the depth, rigor, and resultant learning of mathematical tasks.

This chapter focuses specifically on how to lead the use of ongoing grade-level assessments as part of an interactive process. Mathematics assessment, when led well, serves as a bridge in the teaching-assessing-learning cycle. This is an ongoing cycle of various length—short, medium, and long term—throughout the school year. Teachers *and* students constantly collect evidence of student learning and respond to that evidence using rich and descriptive real-time feedback.

Research That Informs Assessment

Wiliam (2007b) sees assessment as perhaps *the* most important leadership task of the principal:

> Students taught by teachers developing the use of assessment for learning outscored comparable students in the same schools by approximately 0.3 standard deviations, both on teacher produced and external state-mandated tests (Wiliam, Lee, Harrison and Black, 2004). Since one year's growth as measured in the Trends in Mathematics and Science Study (TIMSS) is 0.36 standards deviations (Rodriquez, 2004, p. 18), the effects of the intervention [formative assessment] can be seen to almost double the rate of student learning. (p. 1059)

The highly effective principal understands that *assessment* is no longer defined by and limited to the summative function or purpose of unit assessments, benchmark tests, and high-stakes state assessments. These types of assessments assign grades, scores, and rankings without the expectation, or often even the capacity, to make improvements and adjustments to lesson preparation and design. That impacts student learning and understanding.

High-quality assessment practices, then, integrate *formative* assessment *for* learning (used for making instructional adjustments and student self-reflection for action) with *summative* assessment *of* learning (used for evaluating students' achievement, assigning student grades, and evaluating overall mathematics program success on school, district, state, or provincial benchmark exams).

The National Council of Teachers of Mathematics (2000) explains this relationship clearly:

> Assessment should be more than merely a test at the end of instruction to see how students perform under special conditions; rather, it should be an integral part of instruction that informs and guides teachers as they make instructional decisions. Assessment should not merely be done to students, it should be done for students, to guide and enhance their learning. (p. 22)

During the decade following this declaration, educational experts including Rick Stiggins (2002, 2007), James Popham (2006), and Dylan Wiliam (2007b) cited significant research regarding the impact of formative short-term assessments on overall student learning. In addition, Wiliam, Lee, Harrison, and Black (2004) found that "over the course of a year, the rate of learning in classrooms where teachers were using short- and medium-cycle formative assessment was almost double that found in other classrooms" (p. 49).

Ehrenberg, Brewer, Gamoran, and Willms (2001) report that the impact of assessments for learning on student achievement is four to five times greater than reducing class size. Furthermore, "the true value of assessment is its ability to help educators make accurate and timely inferences about student progress so that they can modify instruction accordingly" (Ainsworth, 2007, p. 80).

When elementary school principals pursue a clear and sustained distinction between assessment *for* learning and assessment *of* learning, there is evidence of a positive impact on student learning and success. Stiggins, Arter, Chappuis, and Chappuis (2006), in *Classroom Assessment for Student Learning*, state, "Few interventions have the same level of impact as assessment *for* learning. The most intriguing result is that while all students show achievement gains, the largest gains accrue to the lowest achievers" (p. 37). The 2008 National Mathematics Advisory Panel report, *Foundations for Success*, used a strict standard of scientific research to recommend improvements in the mathematics education of children K–8. Their exhaustive review of the research discovered only one scientifically based result: "Teachers' regular use of formative assessment improves their students' learning . . . the results are sufficiently promising that the Panel recommends regular use of formative assessment for students in the elementary grades" (p. xxiii).

Visit **go.solution-tree.com/leadership** for further resources regarding assessment.

Formative Assessment Actions

Formative assessment cannot function solely as an accountability measure. Effective school leaders recognize that the skillful use of assessment can benefit teacher and student learning. Assessment *for* learning begins when teams of teachers use classroom assessments and other information sources about student achievement to advance student learning. According to Dylan Wiliam (2007a),

> The big idea of formative assessment is that evidence about student learning is used to adjust instruction to better meet student needs; in other words, teaching is adaptive to the student's learning needs, and assessment is done in real time. More explicitly (Thompson & Wiliam, 2007, p. 6), formative assessment is:
>
> Students and teachers
>
> Using evidence of learning
>
> To adapt teaching and learning
>
> To meet immediate learning needs
>
> Minute-to-minute and day-by-day (p. 191)

A highly effective school principal leads the assessment implementation and analysis of grade-level teachers and teacher teams with several critical questions. When used well, they support the growth of teacher teams toward more coherent assessment practices connected to improved student achievement:

- How well do we understand, in advance of teaching a content unit of study, the student learning targets and the assessments that align with those targets?

- How well do we identify agreed-on scoring rubrics and procedures that will accurately reflect student achievement?

- How well do we use classroom assessments that build student confidence and require students, through goal setting and reflection, to take responsibility for what they know and what they don't know?

- How well do we provide summative assessment results that give frequent, descriptive (versus judgmental) feedback for students, including specific insights regarding strengths and areas of improvement?

- How well do we—as a team—adjust instruction based on the results of both formative and summative classroom assessments?

The described *assessment actions* begin to break down the teacher and administrator belief that assessment is solely about measurement of fixed performance and achievement. Rather, assessment is a tool for learning and improving when the teacher provides the student with feedback that is timely, descriptive, and reflected on. These formative assessment questions are the foundation of an assessment cycle for continuous improvement and growth.

The principal plays the important role of supporting the integration of ongoing formative and summative assessments into this cycle—for both the students and the teacher team.

Designing a Five-Step Assessment Cycle for Continuous Improvement

According to the National Council of Supervisors of Mathematics (2008b), school principals must ensure that "every teacher uses formative assessment processes to inform teacher practice and student learning" (p. 51). When monitoring the assessment work of grade-level teacher teams, principals seek to answer these formative assessment questions:

- How will students express their ideas, questions, insights, and difficulties?

- Where are the most significant conversations taking place (student to teacher, student to student, teacher to student)?

- How approachable and encouraging is the teacher as students explore? Do students see each other as reliable and valuable learning resources?

The summative and formative five-step assessment cycle described in figure 3.1 provides a tool for deep inspection of a principal's assessment expectations. These include the quizzes, projects, and tests that grade-level teams use for unit-by-unit assessment *of* learning for the assignment of grades or mastery scores. The process subsequently turns those summative expectations into formative learning opportunities. In adopting this broader view of the function of assessment, the principal embraces the importance of creating a sustained and systemic assessment process cycle—during instruction. As Wiliam (2007b) indicates, in order to "improve the quality of learning within the system, to be formative, feedback needs to contain an implicit or explicit recipe for future action" (p. 1062).

For an assessment cycle in a grade-level content topic or domain (such as geometry or addition and subtraction of fractions) to be effective, teachers must work in collaborative teams. Grade-level teachers should develop common summative assessments with scoring rubrics in advance of the one- to three-week mathematics unit of study. With this, the learning targets and mathematical tasks are crystal clear to the team. In order to document individual mastery of expected standards (this is the accountability aspect of assessment), the grade-level team works together on four primary tasks that facilitate action on the assessment cycle: (1) determining how to best inform the students of the learning targets, (2) providing students with formative learning opportunities, (3) obtaining student insight for improvement in the target, and (4) helping students self-assess progress on the learning target.

The teacher team then launches the cycle with the implementation of the lesson plans and the necessary assessments designed for a topic or unit of essential mathematics content and

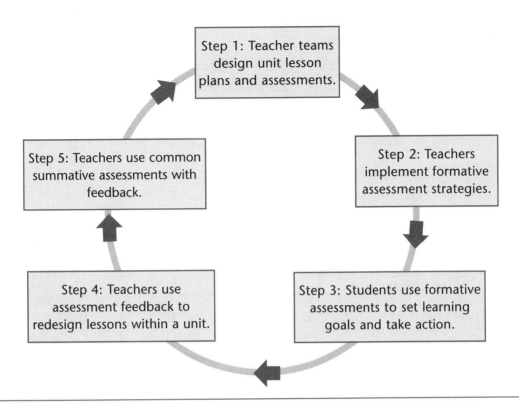

Figure 3.1: The summative and formative assessment cycle.

study. Moving clockwise in figure 3.1, the teachers can make adjustments and move back and forth in the cycle, as needed, giving feedback and using formative assessment tools and strategies. Ultimately, adjustments may be necessary in the lesson plan due to individual student differences. Both the students and teachers reflect on performance during and after the unit. Teachers take notes on what went well, what changes to make, and so forth. The students reflect on successes and next steps. Then the cycle continues again for the next instructional domain or topic.

Thus quality formative assessment during a one- to three-week block of focused mathematics instruction (such as the Measurement and Data content domain) is an ongoing process for students and teachers rather than an occasional event. Whether the assessment is used for grading purposes or not is irrelevant. Every student assessment opportunity is viewed through the lens of a formative assessment opportunity for the student and, for the teacher, as a way to monitor and guide instruction.

It is important to note that although this formative and summative assessment cycle is designed for a one- to three-week unit, there are also the short-term cycles that take place on a day-to-day basis and long-term cycles that last several months, a semester, or a school year (such as a state testing cycle). In the long-term cycles, it is an absolute requirement to use all benchmark assessments to form and adjust student learning and teacher lesson preparation.

Step 1: Teacher Teams Design Unit Lesson Plans and Assessments

For each unit, the grade-level teacher team designs lessons based on three essential assessment agreements: (1) the identified learning targets, (2) the identified common summative assessment instruments, and (3) the identified daily, formative assessments. All teacher formative assessment work during the unit should be based on teacher team understanding and agreement regarding the summative assessment expectations at the end of the unit.

Learning Targets

Teams identify the mathematical concept- and skill-level targets or standards for proficiency, as well as the mathematical understanding–level targets for proficiency. Furthermore, teams determine the CCSS Mathematical Practices that will be evident within this content topic or domain. One of the major benefits of the CCSS for mathematics is the well-identified learning target expectations. The number of learning targets is limited for each grade level in order to allow greater depth and less breadth of topics per grade level. There is, however, a greater expectation for assessing student understanding of the conceptual knowledge necessary for developing procedural knowledge and skills. The following feature box illustrates this with a grade 2 learning target from the CCSS under the domain Number and Operations–Base Ten.

Sample CCSS Grade 2 Learning Targets

Understand Place Value

1. Understand that the three digits of a three-digit number represent amounts of hundreds, tens, and ones; for example, 706 equals 7 hundreds, 0 tens, and 6 ones. Understand the following as special cases:

    a. 100 can be thought of as a bundle of 10 tens—called a "hundred."

    b. The numbers 100, 200, 300, 400, 500, 600, 700, 800, and 900 refer to one, two, three, four, five, six, seven, eight, or nine hundreds (and 0 tens and 0 ones).

    c. Count within 1,000; skip-count by 5s, 10s, and 100s.

2. Read and write numbers to 1,000 using base-ten numerals, number names, and expanded form.

3. Compare two three-digit numbers based on meanings of the hundreds, tens, and ones digits, using >, =, and < symbols to record the results of comparisons.

Source: CCSSO, 2010a, p. 19.

The CCSS define what students should understand, as well as the skills they must be able to do in their study of mathematics. Asking a student to understand something also means asking a teacher to assess whether the student has understood it—and thus, the formative assessment loop begins. A collective team effort to meet the vision of the CCSS "understanding standards" must become part of the formative assessment function during a unit of instruction.

Common Summative Assessments

Based on the identified learning targets for the unit of study, teacher teams determine the common summative assessments the grade-level teacher will use during this unit. They also identify the summative tests and projects that will be used for the purpose of determining a student's grade or mastery level. In addition, they develop scoring rubrics to grade student work on the agreed-on performance targets and designate how these rubrics will be used during the formative assessment process of the unit to provide descriptive feedback to the students and further ensure potential mastery on the summative assessments.

Developing the basis for high-quality summative assessments, along with the grading of those common assessments and common homework assignments, defines a boundary to the expected and common grading practices that all grade-level teams should use.

Daily Formative Assessments

Based on the summative assessments that will be used during the unit, teams determine the daily mathematical tasks needed to ensure students are prepared for the rigor and expectations of those summative tasks. Lesson design preparation takes into account the rigor level of the skill and understanding that the mathematical tasks or problems presented to the students during the unit will require. Step 1 is where inequity can initially appear, depending on task selection and rigor. Equity in mathematics assessment begins with a lesson plan design that uses mathematical tasks of sufficient richness combined with tasks that engage students in observable communication for ongoing formative assessment.

Teachers and teacher teams should spend time connecting the Mathematical Practices—such as "construct viable arguments" and "critique the reasoning of others"—to the design of lessons that teach and assess both procedural knowledge and student conceptual understanding. Honoring the CCSS Mathematical Practices as part of step 1 ensures the opportunity for formative learning and reaps the benefit of increased student learning.

Step 2: Teachers Implement Formative Assessment Strategies

Steps 2 and 3 of the assessment cycle—although serving different functions—occur simultaneously throughout the daily actions of the mathematics unit. Teachers intentionally plan for and implement learning structures, and they provide descriptive feedback that allows this type of formative student reflection to occur. Students take more responsibility for their learning by *reflecting* long enough on their classwork, as well as their formal assessments, to view mistakes as learning opportunities.

Stiggins and colleagues (2006) suggest several strategies of assessment *for* learning during a unit of instruction. The feature box on page 48 lists several of these strategies, which provide insight into the nature of teacher-designed and student-led formative assessments.

Formative Assessment Strategies

Provide a clear and understandable vision of the learning target—Share the learning targets, objectives, or goals with your students in advance of teaching the lesson, giving the assignment, or doing the activity. Provide students with scoring guides written so they can understand them. Develop scoring criteria and rubrics with them.

Use examples and models of strong and weak work—Use models of strong and weak work including anonymous student work, work from life beyond school, and your own work. Begin with work that demonstrates strengths and weaknesses related to problems students commonly experience, especially the problems or tasks that require student demonstrations of understanding.

Offer regular descriptive feedback—Offer descriptive feedback instead of grades on work that is for practice. Descriptive feedback should reflect student strengths and weaknesses with respect to the specific learning target(s) they are trying to hit in a given assignment. Feedback is most effective when it identifies what students are doing right, as well as what they need to work on next.

Teach students to self-assess and set goals—Self-assessment is a necessary part of learning, not an add-on to do if time or with the "right" type of students. Self-assessment includes having students do the following:

- Identify their strengths and areas for improvement for specific learning targets.
- Write in a response log at the end of class, recording key points they have learned and questions they still have.
- Offer descriptive feedback to classmates.
- Use your feedback, feedback from other students, or their own self-assessment to identify what they need to work on and set goals for future learning.

Source: Stiggins et al., 2006.

As teachers plan the unit's mathematics lessons, they can use these formative assessment strategies to inform students about their progress and design activities that allow the students to set action steps for learning based on the formative feedback they are receiving from the teacher and other students.

Assessment, then, is not viewed simply as a final measure of how students perform, but rather as something the teacher does to help students engage in understanding with one another and with the teacher. This understanding centers on where the students need to focus their energy and effort for future work and study.

Step 3: Students Use Formative Assessments to Set Learning Goals and Take Action

According to Wiliam (2007b), feedback, or formative assessment, should draw attention to three key instructional processes:

1. Establishing where the learners are in their learning

2. Establishing where they are going

3. Establishing what needs to be done to get them there (p. 1064)

Students and teachers share the responsibility for successful implementation of formative assessment practices. Students who understand learning targets can reflect on their individual progress toward that target. They can establish learning goals and actions they will take in order to reach the targets. Teachers support students' progress with immediate and effective feedback during classroom conversations.

It is important to understand that the practice "teach students to self-assess and set goals" places much of the responsibility of feedback response and action on the student. Self-assessment is a necessary part of learning. Students need to identify their own strengths and areas for improvement and use teacher feedback, feedback from other students, or their own self-assessment to identify what they need to work on as they set goals for future learning (Stiggins et al., 2006).

Step 4: Teachers Use Assessment Feedback to Redesign Lessons Within a Unit

In this step of the assessment cycle, teachers and teacher teams reflect on their presentation of mathematical tasks. Was there an engaging and formative learning environment? Were there appropriate formative assessment strategies to determine student understanding of the intended learning targets? The following feature box highlights critical questions every grade-level team can use when assessing lesson success and redesigning future lesson plans.

Lesson Planning for Formative Assessment

1. How much of the lesson or material was covered through student exploration or student questioning (instead of didactic lecture)?

   Is there evidence of a climate of mutual respect as students provide meaningful feedback to other students?

   How will students make and test predictions, hypotheses, and estimations with the teacher and with one another?

2. What kinds of in-class formative assessments were used to form the lesson and evaluate the effectiveness of the lesson?

   How did teachers provide descriptive feedback to the students, engage students in the lesson, and develop student interest through the lesson design?

   Were fundamental concepts of the subject taught with evidence of student understanding?

   How did students reflect on their learning as it relates to the learning target?

3. What were the CCSS Mathematical Practices students used to manipulate information, arrive at conclusions, and evaluate knowledge claims?

   Was there evidence that students are part of a learning community?

   How did students communicate their ideas to others?

   How did teacher questions trigger divergent modes of thinking?

4. What kinds of questions and conjectures did students propose in the early stages of the lesson, and what kinds of student-led summative exercises were used to measure student understanding and learning?

Using these questions as part of the teacher lesson plan allows the teacher a greater chance of gathering data during instruction that will inform aspects of the next day's lesson. Thus teachers working with their teams may redesign lessons several times during a unit of study, based on the formative feedback collected during the lesson instruction.

Lesson planning with built-in formative assessment of student understanding is the first tier of a response to intervention (RTI) approach as well. Tier 1 is the single most important aspect of RTI in mathematics. Proponents of the three-tier RTI model suggest that with the right instruction and classroom formative assessment, 80 percent of elementary students' support needs can be met in this first tier. The school's systemic RTI mathematics response discussed in chapter 4 is first and foremost a classroom formative assessment.

Step 5: Teachers Use Common Summative Assessments With Feedback

Wiliam (2007b) clarifies *summative* assessment purposes as monitoring, diagnosing, and formatively assessing learning. He states:

> [A summative] assessment monitors learning to the extent it provides information about whether the student, class, school or system is learning or not; it is diagnostic to the extent it provides information about what is going wrong, and it is formative to the extent it provides information about what to do about it. (p. 1062)

Consider the following scenario. A fourth-grade student takes a summative unit exam on number operations for fractions. He scores 58 percent correct. The class score, or average, is 67 percent. This is the monitoring assessment function. When teachers work within an assessment *cycle*, however, they do not stop here. They use the summative assessment instrument to inform future learning. In this case, a further analysis of the specific student performance indicates that he is not demonstrating success on the learning target "building fractions from unit fractions by applying and extending previous understandings of operations on whole numbers." This is the diagnostic assessment. Often this student is told to try harder or to practice more with decomposing a fraction into a sum of fractions with the same denominator.

A diagnostic assessment is rarely sufficient. Diagnostic assessment does not tell students what they need to do differently (other than try harder). However, only when the teacher uses the summative assessment result to provide feedback for student learning and action does the summative assessment instrument become used for a formative process. For instance, if the teacher uses a visual fraction model to demonstrate $3/8 = 1/8 + 1/8 + 1/8$; $3/8 = 1/8 + 2/8$; $2 1/8 = 1 + 1 + 1/8 = 8/8 + 8/8 + 1/8$, then the summative assessment result has the possibility of being formative for the student, should it help the student to successfully complete the standard the next time it is assessed.

The summative test also becomes formative for the grade-level teacher team if they use the summative assessment results to change teacher instruction for the next instructional topic or unit (a more medium-term loop to inform instruction). This requires the team to write and design common summative assessments in advance of teaching the next unit of instruction.

The following feature box highlights an adapted summative assessment development process for grade-level teacher teams.

Common Assessment Planning Process

Plan—Decide what to assess and how to assess it. How important is this topic? What is the breadth and depth of the learning targets for the topic? Are the learning targets—skill level and understanding level—clear to the teacher team? What will be the role of instructional tools in the assessment?

Develop—Determine the sample questions and tasks for the assessment. Select, create, or modify test items or tasks and scoring rubrics as needed to meet student needs. What will be the format and methods used for student demonstrations of proficiency?

Critique—Evaluate the test for quality. On what basis does the teacher team know it has written a high-quality exam? Does the school have a well-defined and understood set of criteria for writing high-quality unit assessment design?

Administer and grade—Give a unit test or assessment to students and immediately correct it with descriptive feedback. Use the predetermined scoring rubric to grade student work. Ideally, teacher teams grade unit assessments together.

Revise—Evaluate test quality based on results and revise as needed for the following year. Also use the results to inform potential learning target and assessment questions that may need to be repeated as part of the next unit of study.

Source: Stiggins et al., 2006.

The five-step cycle for summative and formative assessment has a powerful impact on student achievement and learning. As Wiliam (2007b) indicates in his research from 2004, "Over the course of a year, the rate of learning in classrooms where teachers were using short- and medium-cycle formative assessment [as part of the summative assessment process] was approximately double" (p. 2).

This cycle for continuous improvement relies on teachers working together in grade-level or grade-cluster teams. More than just becoming masters of teaching content, elementary school teachers must also become masters at using varied assessments. This includes the formative classroom assessment strategies listed in step 2 designed for students to take greater ownership of their learning. As the mathematics unit of study comes to an end, students who have received formative feedback (allowing them to correct errors before the final summative assessment of the content topic or domain) perform at significantly improved rates of learning (Wiliam, 2007b). When the instruction is complete, both the teacher and the student must reflect on the results of their work and use the summative assessment to serve as a formative feedback loop for the next unit.

Avoiding Inequities

When grade-level teachers and leaders work together in a learning community, they serve to erase the inequities caused by the wide variance in student learning and assessment task experiences. Grade-level teachers' isolated decisions regarding the rigor of daily mathematical task selection, daily and unit assessment or task selection, and instructional lesson design practices primarily cause this variance. This is true throughout the mathematics teaching and learning experience. Kanold (2011) cites five general aspects of assessment inequity created by the failure of grade-level teams to work together regarding formative and summative assessment task and instrument creation. If left unchecked, these assessment issues create a vertical deficiency in student learning that widens the mathematics achievement-level gap from year to year:

> Task selection inequity—This applies to the selection and rigor of daily tasks and experiences performed by students each day in class (a quality of lesson planning issue from teacher to teacher).

> Formative assessment inequity—This applies to task selection and level of daily rigor of class prompts teachers use to assess student understanding of various tasks. This applies to variance in rigor and task selection for homework assignments and expectations for make-up work. It also applies to depth, quality, and timeliness of teachers' descriptive feedback on all formative student work.

> Summative assessment inequity—This applies to rigor in task selection that teachers or teacher teams use for unit tests and quizzes. As the school leader, the principal should define high-quality assessments for each academic discipline, grade level, or course. The principal should also determine the level of tolerance for tests and exams that do not meet the prescribed standards, or that hold a wide variance of task rigor from teacher to teacher of the same grade level or course.

> Grading inequity—This applies to any grading of an assessment and the formative learning and feedback loops provided for the students. This creates one of the greatest inequity issues that all grade-level team members must address in discussion for agreement of practice.

> RTI inequity—This applies to the intentional and collective team response to instruction and intervention. The principal should examine how variant, swift, and complete this response is on all aspects of the mathematics programs and determine how well the RTI responses demonstrate evidence that the students and the teachers are becoming reflective learners. (pp. 112–113)

The elementary school principal works hard to ensure grade-level teacher teams attack these inequities, especially the RTI inequity–the intentional and collective teacher team response to instruction and intervention.

Focusing on Large-Scale Assessment

From a policy point of view, the principal in modern schools must focus on large-scale assessments and assessment data. Assessment of student performance plays a critical role in local and district systems, providing consistent measures of whether or not students are meeting or exceeding the district's mathematics standards. Whether doing so enhances student learning in mathematics generates a "both mixed and indistinct" answer, according to the Mathematical Sciences Education Board (MSEB, 1993). Furthermore, "the WYTIWYG phenomena—'what you test is what you get'—is an example of how external assessments can have both good and bad effects on instruction" (p. 151). In order to make sure WYTIWYG does not highlight the bad side of assessment, a principal must remove two primary barriers with respect to large-scale assessments: (1) using direct benchmark tests to serve only a summative function and (2) using large-scale state- or district-level tests that only test low-level procedural knowledge.

First, a principal will address whether district benchmark tests serve only a summative function. It is important for the school principal to understand that district benchmark tests *not* used as a long-term formative assessments quickly become misused summative tests perceived to determine if teachers are keeping up with the curriculum pacing guide. James Popham (2006), quoting Lorrie Shepard, says it best:

> Assessment expert Lorrie Shepard believes that this approach [using benchmark tests only for summative purposes], which is based solely on marketing motives, is corrupting the meaning of the term *formative assessment*, thereby diminishing the potentially positive effect of such assessments on student learning. During the 2006 National Large-Scale Assessment Conference, Shepard observed, "The research-based concept of formative assessment, closely grounded in classroom instructional processes, has been taken over—hijacked—by commercial test publishers and is used instead to refer to formal testing systems called 'benchmark' or 'interim assessment systems.'" (p. 86)

It is the principal's role and responsibility, then, to ensure that such benchmark tests are used for formative functions. As Popham (2006) further indicates, however, there is hope for longer-term, large-scale assessments:

> Properly formulated formative classroom assessments (or even sufficiently short-cycled district assessments) can help students learn better and can improve those students' scores on external accountability tests. Persuasive empirical evidence shows that these tests work; clearly, teachers should use them to improve both teaching and learning.
>
> I am not suggesting that longer-cycle tests, such as the so-called benchmark or interim tests that we often run into these days, are without merit. They quite possibly may enable teachers to make useful longer-term changes in instruction and curriculum. (p. 87)

The more appropriate use of benchmark testing occurs when using the tests for immediate and corrective feedback. The most powerful use of benchmark tests occurs when teachers *form* instruction and students *form and focus* personal targets for relearning based on benchmark results. Without teacher work time built into the benchmark testing process for this formative function, there is no evidence that the benchmarking effort will affect or improve student learning.

Second, when using large-scale state- or district-level tests that only test low-level procedural knowledge, there is a temptation to aim the rigor of local assessments at the level of state-assessment expectations. When the local-assessment rigor is aimed at the state-level mathematics assessments, the aim is too shallow. State tests traditionally focus on low-level procedural skills and do not require student demonstrations of conceptual understanding.

Under the curriculum guidelines of the CCSS, however, a state assessment system must now provide a coherent and consistent system anchored in college- and career-ready expectations. There are two large state consortiums designing state-level common assessments for grades 3–8 and high school. These *common* state assessments will reflect an expanded vision for the specific grade-level content of the CCSS with large-scale assessments that measure beyond the current multiple-choice bubble-in answer sheets. It is the hope and the expectation that these new exams will:

> Improve the quality and types of items included in on-demand tests to create more cognitively-challenging tasks that measure higher-order thinking and analytic skills, such as reasoning and problem solving;
>
> Move beyond a single, end-of-year test to open the door for performance measures and extended tasks that do a better job of measuring important college- and career-ready skills and model exemplary forms of classroom instruction. (CCSSO, 2010b, p. 4)

Two assessment consortia are developing the state assessments for the CCSS: the Partnership for Assessment of Readiness for College and Careers (PARCC) and the SMARTER Balanced Assessment Consortium (SBAC). At the writing of this book, PARCC is a group of twenty-four states committed to building a next-generation assessment system for grades 3 through high school. This system will be anchored by college- and career-ready tests in high school and will include a combination of end-of-year assessments and midyear assessments. The goal is for the system to be computer based. SBAC is a group of thirty states. This system proposes developing adaptive, online tests that include required summative exams combined with performance tasks given through the year and as optional formative exams. Visit **go.solution-tree.com/leadership** for the most up-to-date information regarding these two assessment consortia.

Priorities for Charting Improvement in Mathematics Assessment

As Tate and Rousseau (2007) indicate in "Engineering Changes in Mathematics Education," "Students' opportunities to learn mathematics are influenced by the assessment policies of the local district. Assessment policies often influence the nature of pedagogy in the classroom" (p. 1222).

Principals may overlook this important influence. How you view assessment, as a bridge or part of a teaching-assessing-learning cycle, is directly related to the quality of instruction at each grade level. The following feature box highlights several assessment actions school principals can take to ensure grade-level mathematics teachers become more productive in their work.

Essential Assessment Actions of School Principals

1. Ensure that the local grade-level curriculum aligns with both the conceptual and skill-based content expectations of the CCSS, and ensure that the Mathematical Practices are addressed within every content topic or domain of instruction.

2. Provide immediate and descriptive teacher and student feedback on all large-scale benchmark-type assessments—including state assessments.

3. Encourage ongoing corrections and reflections by teachers and students based on the results of unit-by-unit summative data performance.

4. Disaggregate student performance data as necessary, and ensure solutions are monitored for improving the performance of all students.

5. Ensure teacher demonstrations of classroom formative assessment strategies, such as those discussed on page 48, to determine the impact of formative assessment on day-to-day teaching and its direct connection to student learning opportunities.

6. Align standards with all assessments, and require common grade-level assessments for all mathematics assignments, including homework, tests, and quizzes.

7. Monitor to ensure the depth of grade-level content aligns with the CCSS expectations.

8. Ensure all summative assessments inform a required RTI response from the teacher, the grade-level teacher team, and the school.

9. Ensure the use of teacher-led, high-quality descriptive and timely formative student feedback for all forms of student assessment *of* learning.

10. Ensure student opportunity to learn through the use of a variety of classroom assessment performance tasks and applications, student projects and activities, and additional time allocated to mathematics instruction as needed.

The vision of assessment described in this chapter is not a simple process. It requires sustained attention to teacher and teacher-team professional development, and it requires that all assessments are used for a correct formative purpose of teacher and student reflection.

Chapter 4 provides the important guidance needed on the critical issues involved in a high-quality RTI response as part of steps 3 and 4 in the assessment cycle.

FOUR

HIGH-QUALITY MATHEMATICS RESPONSE TO INTERVENTION

One issue principals face is the daily delivery of a mathematics program that challenges and engages *all* students. The expectation is that *all* means *all*. That is, all children are entitled to a high-quality learning experience every day. All children should be challenged by the mathematics they are learning and should be supported in their learning of this important subject. This chapter explores critical issues in planning response to intervention opportunities for students and examines specific priorities for reflecting on, and sustaining improvement of, your RTI programs in mathematics.

The levels of intervention needed are typically referenced as *tiers*, as depicted in figure 4.1 (page 58). One interpretation of this model is that the day-to-day mathematics classroom learning activities work for about 80 percent of students. The other 20 percent need further interventions to succeed on grade level, and 5 percent of those students need even more intense intervention support—often delivered as one-to-one instruction.

Research That Informs RTI Practice

The position of the National Council of Teachers of Mathematics (NCTM, 2008) relative to equity is clear:

> Excellence in mathematics education rests on equity—high expectations, respect, understanding, and strong support for all students. Policies, practices, attitudes, and beliefs related to mathematics teaching and learning must be assessed continually to ensure that all students have equal access to the resources with the greatest potential to promote learning. A culture of equity maximizes the learning potential of all students. (p. 1)

With NCTM's position in mind, how do you achieve equity in your mathematics program? You expect that all children—regardless of personal characteristics, backgrounds, or physical challenges—will have the opportunity to succeed in mathematics. While this does not mean

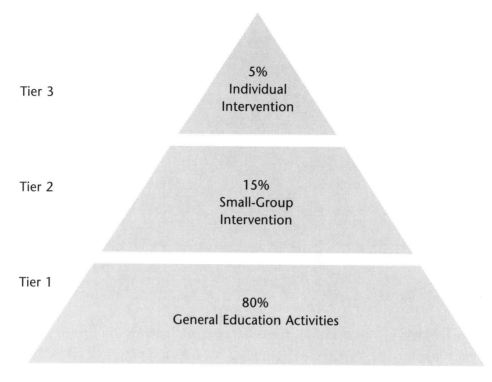

Source: Bender & Crane, 2011.

Figure 4.1: Three-tier RTI pyramid.

all students receive the same instruction all the time, it assumes that "reasonable accommodations are made as needed to help promote access and achievement for all students" (NCTM, 2000, p. 12).

Gersten and colleagues (2009) indicate the following:

> RTI begins with high-quality instruction and universal screening for all students. Whereas high-quality instruction seeks to prevent mathematics difficulties, screening allows for early detection of difficulties if they emerge. Intensive interventions are then provided to support students in need of assistance with mathematics learning. Student responses to intervention are measured to determine whether they have made adequate progress and (1) no longer need intervention, (2) continue to need some intervention, or (3) need more intensive intervention. The levels of intervention are conventionally referred to as "tiers." RTI is typically thought of as having three tiers. Within a three-tiered RTI model, each tier is defined by specific characteristics. (p. 4)

The expectation to provide adequate time and resources for the three tiers of intervention will be a challenge for you and your teachers. You'll need to identify which students need specific accommodations or intervention. You must also decide the accommodations, tiers, and levels of intervention, as well as how you will provide for the delivery of the intervention.

As you think about meeting student needs, recognize that meeting mathematics needs is not a deficit model that focuses on the student as the major source of the problem and ignores

Tier 1 instructional shifts that make a difference. Additionally, many students need to receive a more enriched curricular experience, and some are gifted in mathematics. The challenge of meeting mathematics needs ranges from significant remediation and tiers of intervention to providing access to enrichment opportunities and accelerated programs.

Visit **go.solution-tree.com/leadership** for further resources regarding RTI.

Monitoring Student Performance and Identifying Student Needs

When considering a school's approach to meeting specific student learning needs, the plan is the same regardless of the intervention support; the implementation and next steps are what will vary. The first important steps include the following:

- *Determining instructional needs*—This needs assessment is more than an analysis of state test results and must include day-to-day work, teacher observation and expert opinion, and other formative and summative assessments. A diagnosis should then be framed around important mathematical topics and goals.

- *Adjusting instruction*—Once a diagnosis of instructional needs is determined and documented, considerations for instruction need to be framed. This may include a formal intervention program, before- or after-school support, additional class time for mathematics, and a varying use of curriculum materials and instructional tools, including the use of technology.

- *Monitoring student progress*—Assessing progress is critical. A varied assessment portfolio includes student observation, an analysis of daily classroom contributions, formative assessments, and periodic summative assessments. This should yield a clear indication of student progress and help to guide next steps, instructionally.

As you consider the instructional support or intervention needs of students, the considerations in the checklist in figure 4.2 (page 60) may serve as helpful cues for considering those who need some level of intervention support. Note that the descriptors that follow attend to student learning.

The No Child Left Behind Act (NCLB; the reauthorized and retitled Elementary and Secondary Education Act) requires identification of specific student subgroups. The law indicates that each school and district is assessed to determine if it has achieved adequate yearly progress (AYP) for all students in communication arts and math. In addition, each subgroup is required to meet AYP goals, unless there are thirty or fewer students in the subgroup. These subgroups include the ethnic groups American Indian, Asian, Hispanic, black, and white, as well as students identified in the following ways: limited English proficient (LEP), special education, migrant status, and free and reduced-priced lunch. Since annual test scores for subgroups are used to calculate AYP, you are accountable for all subgroups that populate your school. However, a school must not lower school and classroom expectations of meeting the needs of all students in favor of targeting subgroups, regardless of AYP requirements.

Readiness

    a. Generally proficient with prior concepts and skills _____

    b. Usually needs to review topics _____

    c. Lacks prerequisites _____

Rate of Learning

    a. Seems to be a fast learner _____

    b. Adequate _____

    c. Needs more time than most _____

Attention Span

    a. Stays focused _____

    b. Needs to be told to pay attention _____

    c. Rarely on task _____

Figure 4.2: Checklist of RTI considerations.

Deciding on Accommodations, Tiers, and Delivery of RTI

As teachers identify student needs based on instructional accommodations (from acceleration to intervention), they must provide opportunities to meet such needs. The focus here will be on intervention. Response to intervention has become an important topic for mathematics teachers. RTI has its roots in reading, partially due to the influence of the Reading First initiative. Yet the importance and visibility of annual mathematics state achievement tests for all students in grades 3–8 has created the need for maintaining intervention programs in mathematics. Think of RTI as the opportunity for early detection and prevention of mathematical misconceptions.

Think of RTI as an avenue of ongoing support for students in mathematics. A high-quality intervention program identifies students and provides them with the support they need *before* they fall behind. The Individuals With Disabilities Education Improvement Act (IDEIA, 2004) encouraged states and school districts to use RTI to offer support for students who are having difficulty keeping up with day-to-day expectations in mathematics and thus establishing a need for intervention (Fennell, 2011b).

As teachers use varied assessments to provide the diagnostic screen for determining mathematics needs, instruction must be provided to support and respond to student needs. Follow-up assessments determine whether students have made adequate progress and can either leave the intervention program or continue with it—perhaps changing the time allotted or the tier level based on particular learning needs.

While the number of tiers, or levels, of intervention may vary, the three-tier model noted in figure 4.1 (page 58), with each tier reflecting specific characteristics (Fuchs et al., 2007), is most typical. Tier 1 is classroom-based instruction that aligns with the specific mathematics curriculum topics received by all students in the class. All students are assessed or screened, and particular interventions (such as more time on a concept, use of a particular model, more practice, and so forth) are determined and typically implemented by the classroom teacher and grade-level team.

Students receiving Tier 2 interventions have demonstrated a greater need for targeted assistance in key mathematics concepts. Such interventions may include small-group settings in the classroom or supplemental instruction provided by the classroom teacher and a mathematics specialist or instructional assistant. This additional time for mathematics will vary but may range from twenty to forty minutes, four to five times a week.

Students in need of Tier 3 interventions require more intensive assistance. Such intervention programs are likely to be supplemental and occur outside of the daily mathematics lesson. One-to-one tutoring and additional supplemental support in mathematics tend to be the norm at the Tier 3 level. Special education services and professionals may be involved at this level as the intervention provider, although in some settings the classroom teacher may have this responsibility. At the Tier 3 level, foundational topics (see chapter 1, page 20) must be central to the instructional activities delivered.

While RTI may be considered a by-product of both NCLB and IDEIA, it has become a lifeline for struggling mathematics learners and must be carefully considered and intentionally provided for students in need, regardless of instructional level or how the tiers are defined and addressed within a specific school or district.

Critical Issues for Planning RTI Opportunities

Regardless of the level of need, the principal must consider the same critical questions about how students' mathematics needs will be met:

1. Staffing

    a. How will you staff Tier 3 intervention initiatives? Will this level of intervention occur during the instructional day, as a pull-out program, or before or after the school day?

    b. Will the English learner (EL) specialist, special education faculty, or mathematics interventionist have the mathematics background necessary for implementing a CCSS curriculum, particularly knowing the prerequisite needs of the students?

2. Funding

    a. Will support for RTI initiatives come from Title I, special education funding, or other sources?

b. Are community resources available to support an after-school RTI initiative?

c. Does the school district support specific programs for talented students in mathematics?

Table 4.1 presents a useful planning guide for aspects of the intervention process (Bender & Crane, 2011). This allows the principal or the school's mathematics specialist or instructional leader to account for all aspects of a child's intervention.

When planning for intervention initiatives at the school level, a major focus will be on Tier 1 instruction and Tier 2 intervention needs. Teachers and teacher teams should be entrusted with the planning and implementation details for the intervention opportunities.

Consider the following feature box as a vignette that can be used as a professional development activity related to school-based intervention planning. Teachers should read and react to the plans suggested and consider how they might adapt them for their own purposes.

Primary Level

We decided to use the time after buses arrived, before the beginning of classes, and a slice of time after school for intervention support. In most cases, these were kids who needed catching up, additional practice, or just some one-on-one time to deal with questions they had. Our primary-grade kids worked mostly on addition and subtraction, but we focused on the conceptual background of these operations using problems, which caused the students to represent their solutions using counters or virtual manipulatives. (For example, represent the problem and solution for "Cameron had 7 LEGOs from the collection of 28 LEGOs. Mia had the rest of the LEGOs. How many LEGOs did Mia have?") For each topic we worked on, we preassessed using content-specific items from our county's benchmark test and then gave five-minute check-in assessments at the end of each week, with a longer assessment once a month. This plan seemed to work well with the younger kids (grades 1 and 2).

Intermediate Level

As we began our transition to the Common Core State Standards, we noted that lots of our students did not have the prerequisite background for the beginning work with multiplication and division of fractions that occurs at the fifth-grade level. Our fifth-grade teacher team created a preassessment that focused on whole-number multiplication and division, fraction and decimal concepts, comparing and ordering fractions and decimals, and addition and subtraction of fractions and decimals. The results were not great. They decided that twelve to fifteen students would benefit from significant support on these topics and another seven to eight would need an hour or two of what they called *catch-up time*. Our school's interventionist decided these were, respectively, Tier 2 and Tier 1 needs, with the Tier 1 kids just needing the catch-up time. The teachers worked with the Tier 1 group during recess time three days a week, and the teachers used student interns and our school's Title I math aide to provide the Tier 2 students with half an hour of what they called *math club* four days a week for the entire marking period. The plan seemed to work. It was relatively easy to catch up our Tier 1 kids, and all of them are now ready for the CCSS transition. Our Tier 2 students, for the most part, are thriving with the additional support, and we think many will be ready for our transition to the CCSS. For the others, we will continue our RTI math club and try to connect their prerequisite learning with our new fifth-grade challenges.

Table 4.1: Response to Intervention Planning Grid

	Person Who Implements	Pupil-Teacher Ratio	Curriculum	Intervention Time and Duration	Frequency of Performance Monitoring	Treatment Fidelity Observation	Notifications
Tier 3 More Intensive Instructions							
Tier 2 Targeted Supplemental Instructions							
Tier 1 General Education							

Refer for Special Education

Source: Bender & Crane, 2011, p. 151.

As you think about the team discussions on page 62, consider the following:

1. What are your current actions for your school's Tier 1 and Tier 2 needs?

2. Is there a difference between how you provide intervention for primary and intermediate grade students?

3. Are particular topics at the intermediate level of greater concern than others?

4. What other issues pop for you as you consider the primary and intermediate-level discussions?

Priorities for Charting Improvement in Mathematics RTI

As you consider transition to and implementation of the CCSS regarding intervention, you must consider the Mathematical Practices and the content domains of the Common Core.

CCSS Mathematical Practices and RTI

To ensure that conceptual understanding and problem solving are key partners as curricular essentials for RTI, and within any intervention plan regardless of tier, table 4.2—a slight adaptation to table 1.4 (page 18)—provides the CCSS Mathematical Practices and corresponding student expectations (Fennell, 2011b). This is a glimpse at how students may engage the Mathematical Practices. It is intended to serve as a constant reminder that for each content topic (such as addition and subtraction of whole numbers) or CCSS domain (such as Number and Operations—Fractions), teachers must ensure the Mathematical Practices are integral to the mathematical experiences within any planned intervention program, enrichment plan, or for that matter, an Individualized Educational Plan. The Mathematical Practices and student expectations that follow provide the principal, assistant principal, and school-based mathematics leader with a tool for walkthroughs or informal look-fors regarding student expectations. As indicated in chapter 1, these look-for expectations can be adapted to fit particular content and developmental needs.

Mathematical Content Needs and RTI

Content needs may be determined by teacher observations, use of formative assessments, or use of specifically designed screening assessments. Careful review of the assessment cycle in chapter 3 will provide guidance for using existing assessments and assessment data as teachers intentionally determine content needs for their intervention planning during steps 1 and 2 of the assessment cycle (see page 46).

Once the plan for gathering and using assessment data has been determined, and a plan is in place for the delivery of services, the curricular targets must be determined. Resources such as the Critical Foundations and related benchmarks of the National Mathematics Advisory Panel (2008), the Curriculum Focal Points (NCTM, 2006), or the critical areas of the Common Core State Standards (CCSSO, 2010a). Any of these sources—or an abridged or revised version

Table 4.2: CCSS Mathematical Practices and Student Expectations Related to RTI

Mathematical Practices	Student Expectations
1. Make sense of problems and persevere in solving them.	Students regularly engage in problem solving, and they understand the importance of persevering even when stuck.
2. Reason abstractly and quantitatively.	Students connect observations and responses (for example, drawings and other representations) to mathematical symbols.
3. Construct viable arguments and critique the reasoning of others.	Students regularly discuss approaches and solutions to problems and are comfortable discussing why particular strategies work. They value the contributions and suggestions of their classmates.
4. Model with mathematics.	Students use mathematics to represent solutions and problems—as expressions, equations, or drawings—and they use such representations to determine if their results make sense.
5. Use appropriate tools strategically.	Students have access to and use manipulative materials, drawings, technological tools, rulers, protractors, and other tools.
6. Attend to precision.	Students recognize the need for precision in responding to a problem, coordinating drawings to numerical work, and developing mathematical vocabulary.
7. Look for and make use of structure.	Students look for patterns and structure in the mathematics they are learning. For instance, they are able to compose and decompose numbers, compare and order numbers and amounts, look for patterns, and define a unit.
8. Look for and express regularity in repeated reasoning.	Students have many opportunities to use and then reason about strategies and methods they have learned.

of any of these sources—represent essentials for all students at each grade level. They can serve as a template for the diagnostic screening assessments created and administered for placement purposes. Deciding on particular key elements of the mathematics focus within an intervention plan is important. Less is more—focusing on fewer topics deeply and well and then moving to grade-level expectations should be the content goal.

Table 4.3 (page 66) uses an abridged version of the benchmarks from the Critical Foundations of Algebra of the National Mathematics Advisory Panel report (2008) and, in particular, identifies those benchmarks related to important content standards within the CCSS for the elementary school levels (K–6). The Critical Foundations and CCSS content domains template in table 4.3 provide a checklist to ensure all students have the opportunity to become proficient in these prerequisite critical skill areas. Such considerations should guide the framing of the mathematics essentials determined for any tier within an RTI initiative. Also consider table 1.1 (page 11) as an instrument, which includes all of the CCSS content domains for levels K–6. Table 1.1 offers a domain-based glimpse of all content areas for intervention consideration and allows broad identification of needs, while table 4.3 is more specific with regard to foundational topics and skills.

Table 4.3: National Mathematics Advisory Panel Critical Foundations and Benchmarks

Fluency Attained (provide date)	CCSS Content Domains— Approximate Grade Level	Fluency With Whole Numbers
	4	Addition and subtraction
	5 or 6	Multiplication and division
Fluency Attained (provide date)	**CCSS Content Domains— Approximate Grade Level**	**Fluency With Fractions**
	3 or 4	Identify and represent fractions and decimals and compare them on a number line or with other common representations of fractions and decimals.
	5	Add and subtract fractions and decimals.
	6	Multiply and divide fractions and decimals.
	7	Complete all operations involving positive and negative integers.
Proficiency Attained (provide date)	**CCSS Content Domains— Approximate Grade Level**	**Proficiency With Geometry and Measurement**
	6	Solve problems involving perimeter and area of triangles and all quadrilaterals having at least one pair of parallel sides (such as trapezoids).
	6	Analyze the properties of two-dimensional shapes, and solve problems involving perimeter and area; analyze the properties of three-dimensional shapes, and solve problems involving surface area and volume.

Visit **go.solution-tree.com/leadership** *for a reproducible version of this table.*

Although necessary, these foundational topics and skills are not sufficient; their acquisition is baseline for all Tier 1 instruction and Tier 2 intervention students. The communication and connection-related aspects of the CCSS Mathematical Practices (see table 4.2) should engage students in actually doing mathematics. That said, the actual problems provided for students must resonate with their interests. Consider the following teacher vignette.

> When we began our after-school math club program for our Tier 2 fourth and fifth graders, we let them pick a theme they liked and then we framed problems around that theme. Last month, it was the Baltimore Ravens. Since none of us knew much about the team, we first enlisted them to help us do some research, and they then helped us to pull together all kinds of team and individual player data to help frame problems. (For instance, how much heavier Ben Grubbs was than each student in the group.) The kids couldn't wait to see what Ravens problems they could help us create and solve.

Framing problems around interests may include connections to other areas of mathematics—for example, linking work with fractions to geometry or algebra as well as to other settings. Such settings could include, but certainly are not limited to:

- Science (estimating and measuring mass or weight of various objects all of the same size)

- Sports (determining points scored in a basketball game, calculating various averages, finding the angles for shooting or rebounding a basketball)

- Reading (using story contexts to portray and solve problems)

- Geography (working with maps and coordinates or distances traveled)

It is important to develop and use mathematics problems, or related learning tasks, that involve contexts interesting to the students, particularly with students who need some level of intervention support. This helps nurture student disposition. Students need to like the subject and know how to use it.

Student Communication as Part of RTI

The Mathematical Practice "construct viable arguments and critique the reasoning of others" suggests that students be involved in discussing the mathematics they are learning and write about such experiences. For students who have struggled with mathematics or are beginning to struggle with this subject, this will be a challenge, but one which must be met. Regardless of student placement within a class or the level of intervention being considered or received, ways to help engage students include providing smaller classes or creating small groups within classes and taking the initiative to pull students into discussions, all while remembering to accept and build on their responses.

Consider the following vignette related to a school's plan to meet instructional needs.

We decided to have a pull-out program for kids needing that extra push to catch up in mathematics. We were using the critical areas of the CCSS (CCSSO, 2010a) and connecting those to the benchmarks of the National Mathematics Advisory Panel report (2008) as guideposts for our work. We decided to focus on multiplication and division with third and fourth grades.

Common Core State Standards

Critical areas for grade 3—Develop understanding of multiplication and division and strategies for multiplication and division within 100.

Critical areas for grade 4—Develop understanding and fluency with multidigit multiplication and dividing to find quotients involving multidigit dividends.

Benchmarks for the Critical Foundations

Fluency with whole numbers—By the end of grade 5, students should be proficient with multiplication and division of whole numbers.

We spent a lot of time scrambling for and creating representational models and materials that really focused on understanding multiplication. The students seemed to like using rectangular areas to

continued →

break apart multiplication problems that allowed them to record partial products and actively use the distributive property. So for 28 × 17:

	20	8	
	20 × 10 = 200	8 × 10 = 80	10
	20 × 7 = 140	8 × 7 = 56	7

Our students got really good at using what we called *box multiplication*. We then moved to putting all the partial products together to determine the final product. For our work with division, we used a version of the rectangular region approach, too. We kept up our focus on representing how the operations work before we actually introduced the standard algorithm. We then made sure we had problems to help the kids connect to how the multiplication is used. (For example: We had 17 boxes with 28 small books in each box. How many books were there in all of the boxes?) Our plan of "represent, discuss, and solve" (problems) worked well for us, and the students did well on our weekly checkups. This work helped us think about the transition from conceptual understanding to fluency for our students. Admittedly, our students are not quite fluent, nor are they efficient with their use of a standard algorithm, but finding the developmental trace for multiplication has helped us map a route to fluency—for multiplication—and it really involved the students in creating their own representational models and discussing them with others.

Student Disposition and RTI

Students who are considered for intervention are typically experiencing some level of difficulty with mathematics. The instructional challenge, particularly at the elementary school level, is to determine and provide intervention support that consciously works to improve student achievement and attitude toward mathematics. As a principal, you are more than a moderator of such programs; you're the school cheerleader! No child at the elementary school level should have a negative attitude toward mathematics—that's your mantra! As noted, a particularly important aspect of mathematical proficiency defined in *Adding It Up* (NRC, 2001) is the development and maintenance of a productive disposition. Disposition is indeed important. Students need to like mathematics—and for the most part, they do, early on. Students who perceive themselves as good in mathematics tend to have high levels of achievement (NRC, 2001). However, while many students appear to think mathematics is useful, it is not clear that they think it is important for them to know a lot of mathematics (Swafford & Brown, 1989).

Far too often, the beginning of a negative attitude toward mathematics occurs at the upper elementary and middle grade levels. This is when students begin to proclaim that math is hard. In fact, there was once a Barbie doll who made such a "math is hard" claim. As students move into the behaviors associated with preadolescence, they may even broadly proclaim "math sucks," and Danica McKellar (2007) aims to overturn this with her book, *Math Doesn't Suck!* The book targets middle grade students, particularly young women, and now has its own website (www.mathdoesntsuck.com).

Altering parental attitudes about mathematics may also be necessary. A schoolwide goal should be to keep any parent from saying, "Well, I was never good in math, either." Developing a productive disposition is a key issue in developing mathematics confidence. Whatever a principal does at the school level to meet student needs must include shaping each student's mathematical disposition. Making math cool, fun, and important for every student is a particularly important declaration as schools strive to identify and meet student intervention needs, which include content and affective needs. The disposition-related questions in the following feature box can help you, your teachers, and your grade-level teams focus on shaping disposition at the school level.

Shaping Mathematics Disposition

- Are students engaged in the mathematics they are learning?

- Are the problems and activities you provide interesting? Would you want to do them?

- When the emphasis of the lesson or activity is developing or maintaining skills, do the students understand why such work is important?

- Do teachers value student products and comments?

- Are students assisted, praised, encouraged, or pushed when needed?

- Does your school exhibit mathematics work? Projects?

- Does the school have a math club?

- Does the school engage parents to assist in math class?

- Are there math nights to show off the subject and student projects?

- Are local math experts, or people who use mathematics (engineers, florists, lawn services, statisticians, and so forth), brought in to talk about the importance of mathematics?

The first four chapters of the book have provided important considerations for a high-quality school-based mathematics program. These chapters provided considerations and sample plans, activities, and vignettes that should help meet the challenges related to issues in the field of mathematics education, mathematics content, instruction, assessment, and intervention.

It's time to introduce areas of your influence that will determine whether or not the plans that were seeded in chapters 1–4 can actually work. Our discussion now moves to the impact and importance of teacher evaluation, professional development, and your work with families and the larger community. These three topics, as they relate to the school's focus on mathematics teaching and learning, are the principal's responsibility. They provide a regular "report card" of your mathematics program progress.

FIVE
MONITORING, EVALUATING, AND IMPROVING INSTRUCTION

Observing and monitoring high-quality instruction is a major responsibility of the elementary school principal. You are the person ultimately responsible for the quality of instruction your students receive. Although formal observations and evaluation ratings are frequently governed by district, state, or provincial regulations, such ratings—used as summative assessments of instruction—often have a limited impact on changing teacher classroom behavior.

Effective monitoring and supervision of instruction, however, are much more important as principals engage each teacher and team in a collaborative effort to create a cycle of ongoing observation, consultation, and reflection for the purpose of improving each individual teacher's mathematics instruction. In other words, you should use teacher observation as a *formative* assessment aspect of instruction. This chapter addresses how to effectively use observation and feedback formatively: what to look for, how to engage teachers in productive discussions about their practice, and how to work with mathematics content specialists (academic coaches, specialists, and district content leaders) in observing and supporting instruction in your school.

Viewing Teachers as Learners

Research described in chapter 2 (such as Bransford et al., 2000) indicates that learning (including adult learning) is an active process of meaning making; knowledge is socially constructed through talk, activity, and interaction around meaningful problems and timely feedback. This process enables the learner to revise work, thinking, and understandings and to develop reflective awareness as a learner, thinker, and problem solver. This reflective process has important, and specific, implications for the monitoring and supervision of teachers (Nolan & Francis, 1992):

- Teachers should be viewed as active constructors of their own knowledge about learning and teaching. Just as teachers can't simply pour knowledge into the heads of learners, leaders cannot pour instructional knowledge and practices into the heads of teachers. Teachers are learners who must be given the time and opportunity to work with new concepts and practices and relate them to their own prior knowledge and experience. As Nolan and Francis (1992) note, "The primary purpose of supervision [is] *the improvement of teaching and learning by helping teachers acquire a deeper understanding of the learning-teaching process*" (p. 52). This also means teachers should be active participants in the improvement process and should have ongoing opportunities to analyze their own teaching, deliberate with colleagues about their teaching, and confer with the principal and other administrators about their teaching (Kanold, 2007).

- Supervisors should be viewed as collaborators in creating knowledge about learning and teaching. In this view, the supervisor takes an inquiry, rather than a critical stance, and engages teachers in conversations that help them reflect on their practice and its impact on students' learning.

- Data collection should expand from reliance on pencil-and-paper observation instruments of a single period of instruction to include a variety of data sources over time.

The student learning that results from effective lesson design determines the instructional quality. To adequately capture a teacher's instructional practice, information from a variety of data sources is needed in addition to observations of classroom teaching, including the teacher's:

- Goals and expectations for student learning and achievement

- Plans for achieving the student goals

- Sample lesson plans, student activities and materials, and means of assessing students' understanding of mathematics

- Evidence of students' understanding of mathematics

- Participation in collaborative activities with colleagues

Critical Guidelines and Tools for Teacher Observation

Good and Dweck (2006) note that although a variety of data sources are important, observations of classroom teaching are central to improving teaching and learning. Effective colleague and administrator observation of mathematics classes involves going beyond observing the physical and behavioral elements of the classroom to addressing the mathematics teaching and learning occurring.

Chapters 1 and 2 described mathematics teaching as the product of interactions among students, teacher, and content. This view of teaching and the nature of the CCSS Mathematical Practices as student behaviors require the principal to monitor and observe what the teacher *and* students are doing during the lesson. The Mathematical Practices provide concrete expectations for teacher and student classroom behaviors.

Informal observations and walkthroughs can identify whether teachers are using instructional strategies that promote students' development of the practices. The look-fors presented in figure 5.1 (page 74) were created by the Elementary Mathematics Specialists and Teacher Leaders Project (Fennell, 2011b). The targeted observations are not intended to establish all the ways in which the CCSS practices may play out in the classroom; rather, they serve as discussion starters in setting the expectations for their use. In fact, the project website now continues this work with a drop-down menu of both student and teacher expectations for the Mathematical Practices (www.mathspecialists.org).

Another complementary approach is to use the features of high-quality mathematics instruction to identify classroom observation. Admittedly, mathematics teaching is complex; there is a lot to look for, and clearly a principal can't seek all the features within a single class period. Instead, you should identify one or two foci for each observation.

There are a few broad-brush things to look for in any mathematics lesson:

- Who is doing the mathematical thinking—teachers, students, or both?

- What is the goal of the instruction—understanding mathematics or simply getting answers?

- What is the cognitive demand of the tasks students are being asked to do? What happens to the demand as teachers introduce the task, and as students work on the task?

- To what extent are *all* students engaged in mathematics learning?

Figure 5.2 (page 75), the Monitoring and Observation Guide, is based on the description of high-quality mathematics instruction provided in chapter 2. Adapted from the *Lenses on Learning* observation guide (Grant et al., 2006) and the NCTM *Standards for the Observation, Supervision and Improvement of Mathematics Teaching* (Kanold, 2007), the guide provides specific questions to ask about three interdependent dimensions of mathematics classrooms: (1) mathematics content; (2) learning and pedagogy, including formative assessment; and (3) intellectual community. For each dimension, it describes what to look for when observing students and teachers. Note that indicators of students developing proficiency in the CCSS Mathematical Practices are integrated into each of the three dimensions.

The observation tools provided in figures 5.1 and 5.2 are specifically designed to support a formative observation-improvement process, not formal evaluations. They are intended to spark questions and issues for you to discuss with the teacher, for the teacher to discuss with the grade-level teacher team, and for the instructional mathematics specialist or coach to provide support. They are most useful when the focus of observation is on one or two cells, and they can be used as part of the preconference, observation, and postconference sequence.

Teacher's Name: _____
Mathematics Leader's Name: _____
Mathematics Domain: _____ Standard: _____
Number of Students in the Class: _____ Date: _____
Length of Time in the Classroom: _____
Grade Level: _____ School: _____

Observed	Mathematical Practices	Lesson Focus
	Make sense of problems and persevere in solving them. 1. Students: Are engaged in solving problems 2. Teacher: Provides time for students to discuss problem solutions	
	Reason abstractly and quantitatively. 1. Students: Are able to contextualize or decontextualize problems 2. Teacher: Provides appropriate representations of problems	
	Construct viable arguments and critique the reasoning of others. 1. Students: Understand and use prior learning in constructing arguments 2. Teacher: Provides opportunities for students to listen to or read the conclusions and arguments of others	
	Model with mathematics. 1. Students: Analyze relationships mathematically 2. Teacher: Provides contexts for students to apply the mathematics learned	Comments
	Use appropriate tools strategically. 1. Students: Use technological tools to deepen understanding 2. Teacher: Uses appropriate tools (such as manipulatives) instructionally	
	Attend to precision. 1. Students: Based on a problem's expectation, calculate with accuracy and efficiency 2. Teacher: Emphasizes the importance of precise communication	
	Look for and make use of structure. 1. Students: Look for patterns 2. Teacher: Provides time for applying and discussing properties	
	Look for and express regularity in repeated reasoning. 1. Students: Regularly check the reasonableness of their results 2. Teacher: Encourages students to look for and discuss regularity in reasoning	

Leader's Signature: _____

Teacher's Signature: _____

Source: Fennell, 2011b. Used with permission.

Figure 5.1: Tool for observing the CCSS Mathematical Practices.

Students	Notes	Teachers
Focus Questions		**Focus Questions**
Mathematics Content What mathematical ideas and standards are students working on during the lesson? What makes the lesson tasks worthwhile mathematics? Is the task appropriate for the mathematical goals of the lesson? • Appropriate level of cognitive demand • Appropriate for students • Requires use of CCSS Mathematical Practices **Learning and Pedagogy** What kind of mathematics sense making are students doing? How are students using their prior knowledge to make sense of the task? In what ways are students making connections among mathematical concepts? How are students using a variety of representations for their mathematical thinking? What mathematical ideas seem to be confusing to students? In what ways are the students visibly developing their mathematical ideas over time? How do students use feedback to modify their thinking? **Intellectual Community** How are students showing respect for one another's ideas? How do students use each other as resources as they make sense of mathematical ideas? What evidence beyond raised hands is there that all students are engaged? In what ways are students listening and reacting to others' thinking and solutions to problems?		**Knowledge of Mathematics Content** What does the teacher seem to understand about the mathematics? What is the teacher's understanding of tasks and how do they represent the mathematical ideas and standards? What does the teacher seem to understand about the development of children's ideas in these standards? What does the teacher seem to understand about children's development in the CCSS Mathematical Practices? **Enactment of Learning and Pedagogy** What is the level of cognitive demand of the task posed? What happened to the level of cognitive demand as the teacher introduced the task? As the students work on the task? How does the teacher work with the sense the children are making? How does the teacher attend to all students? How does the teacher adjust teaching based on the ideas from students? What feedback does the teacher provide to students? How does the teacher debrief the task and engage students in discourse that makes the mathematics visible to all? **Facilitating Intellectual Community** How does the teacher support students in showing respect for one another's ideas? How does the teacher set the tone so students see each other as resources for mathematical thinking? What interventions does the teacher use to ensure students' engagement is focused on mathematical ideas?

Visit go.solution-tree.com/leadership for a reproducible version of this figure.

Figure 5.2: Monitoring and observation guide.

In addition to these two figures, there are two other general aspects of classroom observation that can also provide valuable information for you and the grade-level teacher teams: (1) observing the classroom for equity and (2) observing the classroom as a learning environment.

Observing the Classroom for Equity

Tallying indicators of quality participation for each student (for example, opportunities to respond, type of feedback received, and what type of questions the teacher asks students) provides teachers with powerful data about the extent to which they are engaging *all* students in mathematics learning. Particularly important are the data that highlight patterns in engagement of different student subsets: race, socioeconomic status, gender, or location in the classroom. Teachers sometimes have subconscious biases in their classroom interactions. Information about which students they are or aren't engaging is often very surprising for teachers ("I had no idea I only called on students sitting on the left-hand side of the room.") and instantly makes them aware of changes needed in their practice. This type of observation is a key component of the Teacher Expectations Student Achievement (TESA) program (Gewertz, 2005; Marzano, 2003).

Observing the Classroom as a Learning Environment

The physical appearance of the classroom can also provide important clues about the extent to which rituals and routines are in place to support the class as an intellectual community. This type of function suggests that high-quality instruction is regularly occurring. Look-fors include the following:

- Arrangement of student seating
  - Do students sit at desks organized into rows?
  - Are desks pushed together to form pairs or small groups for learning?
  - Do students sit at group tables instead of desks?
- Availability of tools, such as markers, rulers, tape, calculators, scissors, manipulatives, and graph paper
  - Are these tools readily available to students? (For instance, is there a tool bin on every table or are tools stored so they are accessible to every student all the time?)
- Visual displays to support students' learning
  - Are standards and objectives posted?
  - Are there artifacts that support students' mathematics work (for example, class-generated posters of criteria for good work or problem-solving strategies)?
  - Is student work posted with rubrics? Does the posted work meet the standard, show a variety of solutions, and validate student effort and accomplishment?
  - Does the class have a word wall that highlights important mathematics vocabulary?

- Are visual tools (such as number lines or hundreds charts) posted, and if they are, are they in a location that students can easily see, reach, and use?

Do note that the physical appearance of a classroom is a limited indicator of what is actually happening in instruction. Sometimes teachers post items simply because they are on a look-for checklist. The essential question is whether these items are being used as intended. You should check to determine whether students know what these artifacts are and know how to use them as they *do* mathematics. Taking a minute to ask a student, "Can you tell me what that poster is? How do you use it when you're working on math?" can provide valuable information about the actual purpose and function of posted materials and the classroom learning environment.

Observation Process

Walking in "cold" to observe a lesson provides limited information and understanding about a teacher's instructional practice or the intent of the practice that day or week. While there are times when it makes sense to drop in unannounced to observe instruction, pre-observation conferences provide more detailed information about important aspects of teachers' instructional practices that are not as observable, such as their mathematical goals for the lessons, why they structured the lessons the way they did, and what they expect students to experience.

Pre-Observation Conference

A pre-observation conference provides evidence about the teachers' understanding of the mathematics in the lesson and their expectations for students' learning of that mathematics. Discussing the lesson can also help teachers see lesson-design weaknesses they might not realize when planning the lesson in isolation. The following feature box provides a list of suggested pre-observation questions. These questions are also useful as part of the grade-level team discussions. Examining the teachers' edition of the instructional materials during the conference can provide helpful background information about the lesson's content and intended pedagogy.

Pre-Observation Conference Questions

In order to help you make sense of what you will be seeing when you do your classroom observations, plan to meet with the teacher prior to the observation, and ask the following questions:

1. What mathematical concepts, skills, and practices will you and your students be working on in this lesson? How is this related to CCSS (or state or provincial standards)?

2. What do you plan to do in this lesson (for instance, the origin and structure of the lesson, the tasks you will be using, and so on)?

3. What do you hope to accomplish in this lesson? What do you want your students to leave with?

4. What mathematical ideas are embedded in this lesson?

5. What have you and your students been working on prior to this lesson?

---

continued →

6. How does this lesson fit into your overall goals for this unit? For the year?

7. Are there students who have special needs in this class? What will you do to support their engagement in the lesson?

8. What are you currently working on in terms of improving your instruction?

9. Is there any aspect of your instruction that you would like me to focus on in my observation?

Source: Adapted from Grant et al., 2006, p. 35.

It is important to ask if there is anything the teachers would like you to focus on during the observation. Teachers may be working on improving a particular aspect of their practice, such as questioning, engaging students, or summarizing the learning. Principals should support a teacher's self-refection of performance and perceived areas of need for improvement.

Observation

Key features to monitor while observing the lesson are the level of cognitive demand of the task and how the teacher's implementation affects that level of demand. In particular, if your instructional materials feature lessons that incorporate high-cognitive demand tasks, look for changes in the teacher's design of the lesson compared to the design described in the teachers' guide. In a large-scale study of teachers' use of instructional materials that contained high-cognitive demand tasks, Weiss and Pasley (2004) found that teacher-adapted lessons were less likely to provide high-quality learning opportunities than ones that were taught as the teachers' guide suggested. This is not to say that deviating is not acceptable. In the postconference, it will be important to ask why the teacher changed the lesson design. Be especially aware, however, of responses that communicate low expectations, such as, "My students are lower level, so I changed the task to make it easier for them."

To obtain a complete picture of a teacher's instruction, it is important to see how the teacher closes the lesson (engages students in a discussion of the tasks, their work, and what they learned from their work that day), not just how the teacher sets up the lesson. Weiss, Pasley, Smith, Banilower, and Heck (2003) found that teachers frequently run out of time during lessons that feature high cognitive–demand tasks, thus the debriefing and summary occur the day after students did the original task. Whenever possible, observe the end of the lesson, even if it means a second visit to the classroom the next day.

Postobservation Conference

The postobservation conference is the opportunity for you and the teacher or colleagues to engage in a reflective discussion about instructional practice. Teachers need the opportunity to discuss their perceptions first—strengths, trouble spots, and classroom actions they would do differently in subsequent lessons. Whenever possible, the discussion should build on the teacher's personal reflection and assessment comments. You can do this by asking inquiry questions rather than immediately making suggestions. It is important to focus on one or two features of the lesson (such as level of student engagement, the nature of teacher questioning, and so on) and how teachers might improve on those lesson features. It is not necessary to provide specific suggestions for how to improve; the point is that through discussion, the teacher is encouraged to generate ideas. The collaborative discussion with the teacher is the vehicle for co-constructing productive next steps for improvement.

Priorities for Working With a Mathematics Specialist or Coach

Many schools and school districts now recommend and use mathematics coaches, specialists, and instructional leaders at the elementary school level. The use of such specialists helps schools and school districts ensure that all students receive high-quality mathematics instruction from teachers with a deep understanding of mathematical content and pedagogy. Major reports frequently referenced through this book make such a recommendation, including *Principles and Standards for School Mathematics* (NCTM, 2000), *Adding It Up* (NRC, 2001), *Mathematical Education of Teachers* (CBMS, 2001), and *Foundations for Success* (NMAP, 2008). Furthermore, the combination of the CCSS and the reauthorization of the Elementary and Secondary Education Act (formerly NCLB) now increases the need for continuing support of mathematics professional development through the use of mathematics content specialists in schools.

The term "elementary mathematics specialist" is used to describe a variety of roles, including teachers who only teach mathematics at one or more grades in a departmentalized model. This initiative also includes teachers with specialized preparation in mathematics (similar to reading specialists), who may still teach all content areas, and mathematics coaches—teachers released from teaching duties either full or part time to support their colleagues in improving their mathematics instruction. Specialists typically have a supporting, rather than an evaluative role, in improving instruction; however, they can be valuable partners for principals in the formative observation-conferring-reflection process.

Mathematics content specialists and coaches can assist the elementary school principal to achieve the urgent and essential pursuit to close the gap between knowledge of strategies that produce high-quality instruction and their implementation. In gap-closing schools, teachers work collaboratively and interdependently within the context of their workplace and learn from one another; they participate in professional communities with other mathematics leaders outside their schools and are expected to implement the content of the ongoing professional development. The elementary specialist or coach can be an important leader in the school's professional community, supporting teachers in their classrooms and in team meetings as they work to improve their practice.

Reys and Fennell (2003) present a robust case for the appropriate use of elementary school mathematics specialists:

Why do we need mathematics specialists at the elementary school level? A student's view of what it means to know and do mathematics is shaped in elementary school; yet in the United States, elementary teachers are, for the most part, generalists. Their pre-service teacher education typically includes two or three courses in mathematics content and one course in the teaching of mathematics. Their teaching load generally consists of a full range of subjects, with particular attention to reading or language arts in a self-contained classroom. A mathematics specialist is needed because the pre-service background and general teaching responsibilities of elementary teachers do not typically furnish the continuous development of specialized knowledge required for teaching mathematics today. (p. 277)

There are emerging data that mathematics coaches make a difference in student achievement. The Boston Public Schools have seen significant increases in elementary mathematics achievement with implementation of a standards-based mathematics curriculum, a comprehensive professional development program, a strong formative assessment system, and school-based mathematics coaches (Grant & Davenport, 2009). In a three-year randomized control study, Campbell and Malkus (2011) found that coaches positively affected student achievement in grades 3, 4, and 5, but not until the second and third years of the placement as "coaches gained experience and as a school's instructional and administrative staffs learned and worked together" (p. 430). Furthermore, the coaches in this study had significant preparation in university courses that addressed mathematics content, pedagogy, and coaching prior to and during at least their first year of placement as part of the Virginia Mathematics Specialists Project.

While it's tempting to think of a math coach as someone to whom you can delegate support of mathematics teaching and learning in order for you to take care of other responsibilities, schools make the most progress when principals work closely with their coaches to improve teacher and teacher team mathematical knowledge and practice (Grant & Davenport, 2009).

Based on their work in Boston, Grant and Davenport (2009) identify a number of important ways a principal can work with a mathematics coach or specialist. While some of these ways are discussed in the next chapter on professional development, here are the most relevant ones:

- Work with the mathematics coach to set priorities. This includes setting up regular meetings with the coach to monitor progress and needs and attending grade-level team meetings focused on mathematics.

- Jointly conduct classroom observations and pre- and postconferences with your mathematics coach. Such collaborations help reveal what is happening in classrooms and will develop your eye for mathematics instruction.

- Be strategic about putting support structures in place to strengthen instruction and student learning. This includes scheduling opportunities for the coach to work with grade-level teams of teachers, not just individuals. For example, schedule time for teacher teams to jointly plan a grade-specific lesson; then provide substitutes or coverage so team members can observe each other teach the same lesson and debrief with the coach.

Finally, resist the temptation to assign your mathematics specialist or coach administrative duties beyond supporting mathematics instruction and assessment in the classroom. Academic coaches are most valuable when they use their knowledge and skills as mathematics teachers to improve the instructional and assessment practices of individual teachers as well as the grade-level teacher team.

While the observation-conferring-reflection process is a major tool for principals to improve mathematics instruction, it is only one component of the comprehensive professional development program that is essential for obtaining schoolwide improvement in mathematics teaching and learning—meaning every teacher at every grade providing high-quality instruction for every student.

The new paradigm for the professional development of mathematics teachers requires an understanding that the knowledge capacity of every teacher matters. More important, however, is that every teacher and teacher team *acts* on that knowledge and transfers the professional development they receive to their daily classroom practice.

The next chapter provides specific recommendations for designing and implementing highly effective professional development for your school.

SIX

DESIGNING EFFECTIVE PROFESSIONAL DEVELOPMENT

A fixed set of routine skills and arbitrary rules often characterize classroom learning experiences. Prior to the Common Core State Standards, Stigler and Hiebert (1999) pointed out that mathematics classroom instruction frequently followed a predictable script: (1) review previous material, (2) demonstrate how to solve problems for the day, (3) practice problems, and (4) correct seatwork and assign homework. This script reflected the traditional orientation of mathematics teaching in which students spent most of their time acquiring isolated skills through repeated practice.

The future vision and demands of the CCSS expectations, as well as the research on best practice for highly effective mathematics teaching and learning, call for instruction that is very different from current reality. Most noticeably, all grade-level teachers will be expected to teach for meaning and understanding rather than relying solely on procedural and rote memorization of mathematical concepts. The CCSS Mathematical Practices demand this paradigm shift as an everyday classroom occurrence. For this to happen, however, your school must establish a strong professional development mindset and system that provide every teacher with the confidence and pedagogical knowledge necessary to improve their mathematics teaching and assessing.

While it will take creative involvement on your part to encourage and persuade all teachers to change their pedagogical and assessment style, the effort will lead to higher levels of student engagement, understanding, and learning. As Neuman and Mohr (2001) suggest, the principal's role is to "acknowledge [teachers'] fears, to gently remind them that the old way was not working, and to keep moving forward" (p. 47).

The mathematics professional development of administrators, teachers, and specialists should act as the bridge that connects daily teacher classroom practice to ongoing research in mathematics education. The mathematics teaching and learning vision, along with the expectations of the CCSS, is steeped in a strong foundation of research for how students are to learn and experience mathematics content knowledge development. How well teachers come to know the relevant research and best practice instruction and assessment in mathematics will directly correlate with how well elementary school students perform. It will be the responsibility of teachers and school administrators to mutually identify and undertake a coherent professional development experience that leads to effective action and practice.

A Vision for Mathematics Professional Development: Coherence and Focus

An emphasis on student learning combined with a laser-like focus on teacher knowledge-capacity development is the new paradigm for future professional development in mathematics. The most important future professional development role of the elementary school principal is the relentless pursuit of coherence in the professional development efforts of the school. Deciding the specific mathematics content focus for professional development efforts is a large part of the principal's job as well. Yet for sustainability purposes, principals must focus on the process of how professional development occurs. Current typical modes of professional development for elementary school teachers include the following:

- Individual reading, study, and research in isolation from others

- Grade- or course-level teacher learning teams

- Coaching that uses an expert teacher

- Mentoring for new teachers

- Faculty department meetings

- Online courses

- Peer observation through lesson study

- Workshops provided by the district

- Workshops provided by a mathematics organization

- Whole-school improvement programs

The list goes on: the professional development modes or processes that bombard the classroom teacher can be overwhelming. This is especially true if the various modes focus on different and sometimes conflicting content messages.

Research does not support professional development that relies on one-shot workshop models, that is strictly provided outside the context of the teachers' work environment, or that nurtures an expectation of teacher isolation without support or pressure for implementation (Darling-Hammond & Richardson, 2009). Professional development is not an event or training, as in the old paradigm. At its best, professional development and learning is an ongoing, continuous, sustainable activity inside and outside of the school walls. In fact, "professional development lasting 14 or fewer hours showed no effect on [teacher] learning. The largest effects were for programs offering 30 to 100 hours spread out over 6 to 12 months" (p. 49).

Even thirty to one hundred hours of on-site professional development has diminished effects when it is disconnected from daily teacher classroom work. Variance in teacher subject knowledge is evident when teachers ask what the role of number sense and quantity is or how to teach computation with understanding; how to teach algebra, geometry, functions, and statistics; how to teach vocabulary to EL students; or how to teach for meaning and understanding.

K–8 teachers must address a broad range of content knowledge in mathematics:

- The role of number sense, counting, and manipulative materials
- The role of language and its impact on early mathematics learning
- The implications of children's informal mathematics concepts about size, shape, and space, as well as number and chance
- The role of calculators and computers
- The role of variable and function
- The role of probability and statistics in K–8 mathematics

Add to this list the issues that surround formative assessment cycles, both informally and formally, and faculty and staff will likely begin to feel overwhelmed.

Too often, professional development for mathematics feels disconnected, disjointed, and overwhelming for K–8 teachers. Hayes Mizell (2010), in *Why Professional Development Matters*, indicates, "The effectiveness of professional development depends on how carefully educators [principals] conceive, plan and implement it. There is no substitute for rigorous thinking and execution" (p. 10). The paradigm for teacher professional development has shifted. *Less is more* is the new theme in mathematics for both the content and the process of professional development. In addition, the principal must lead this subtle but important shift—especially in light of the CCSS expectations for more depth with student understanding on fewer learning targets and less breadth with memorization in the mathematics curriculum.

Three Process Issues for Designing Professional Development in Mathematics

In order to build teacher knowledge capacity and sustain implementation of that knowledge into the classroom, the professional development process should be framed around three critical agreements: (1) teacher collaboration, (2) adequate time, and (3) equity and access.

Teacher Collaboration

In this new and emerging paradigm, the term *professional development* means "a comprehensive, substantiated, and intensive approach to improving teachers' and principals' effectiveness in raising student achievement" (NSDC, 2008, p. 6). This new professional development model envisions mathematics teachers and specialists collaborating interdependently to deepen their knowledge of mathematics pedagogical content and competencies; the new paradigm also expects action on that knowledge with application to practice.

Teachers then reflect collaboratively on the impact of their new knowledge for student learning based on the practical application within their classroom actions and experiences. Principals play a crucial role by bringing a coherent focus to the mathematics professional development for teacher knowledge capacity and learning and by limiting the amount of new knowledge the team will pursue in a given year.

Creating a mindset and culture of teacher collaboration is a requirement for sustainable professional development. Schmoker (2005) points out that extensive evidence from the research community indicates unequivocally that the "right kind of continuous, structured teacher collaboration improves the quality of teaching and pays big, often immediate, dividends in student learning" (p. xii). Sowder (2007) notes that teacher communities of practice—that is, teacher teams working together to professionally develop one another—"create, expand, and exchange knowledge about their practice," which in turn leads to a more authentic and subsequent change in actual classroom practice (p. 186). Additional research has also repeatedly concluded that teacher isolation has adverse consequences for students, for teachers, and for any effort to improve schools (DuFour, DuFour, & Eaker, 2008).

Highly effective professional development design in your school must be built on a foundation of school-based teacher learning teams. Leinwand (2009) describes the importance of this collaborative mindset as part of the way professional development must occur: "People can't do what they can't envision, and people won't do what they don't understand, therefore colleagues help each other to envision and understand . . . admitting the need to grow is a core aspect of being a professional" (p. 85). Acting on that need to grow is essential.

Mizell (2010) describes the critical importance of collaboration as the most fundamental way teacher professional development takes place:

> All educators [faculty and administration] are organized into learning teams. Each team has a skilled facilitator to guide the team in establishing and pursuing [student] learning goals. Teams meet during the workday at their school two to three times per week. . . . In team learning, less experienced educators interact with and learn from more experienced educators on the team. As all educators on the team become more skillful, they reduce or eliminate the variations in performance and begin to take collective responsibility for the success of all students, not just their own. (p. 11)

This new paradigm expects elementary school principals to become more involved in mathematics professional development. Spillane's (2005) research highlights another subtle paradigm shift. The school administration must become involved in the learning and growth that mathematics professional development routines generate. Administrators must also provide feedback and support to the implementation expectations of the professional development.

Adequate Time

A second design issue is the provision of adequate time for professional development. Advocating for and ensuring quality time for collaborative teacher learning within a mathematics course (mostly in grades 6–8) or mathematics instruction (mostly in grades K–5) is the responsibility of the school leader. Finding ways to make more effective use of the time currently available within the school culture and seeking ways to enhance time available—as part of the teachers' workday—is essential.

Time is often the toughest challenge principals and teachers encounter as they attempt to fit professional development activities into the already-crowded school schedule. Yet professional development must be given adequate time and take place in school as part of the workday. Teaching children mathematics is a complex activity that is learned through knowledge sharing, coaching, and field-based experience. Teachers as professionals need time to reflect on the success and failures of their daily lessons and weekly assessments with others who are working toward similar grade-level or course goals.

Loucks-Horsley, Love, Stiles, Mundry, and Hewson (2003) outline several approaches that have been used to create more time for professional development:

- Use currently available time more efficiently for collective teacher sharing.

- Use substitutes or early release time for students. Some schools are effectively using one morning or afternoon a week for teacher development and improvement activities by changing the school's daily schedule once per week.

- Purchase teacher time by compensating for after-school, weekend, and summer work.

- Schedule time by providing common planning time for teachers who work with the same children or teach the same grade on a regular basis.

- Restructure time by permanently altering teacher responsibilities, the teaching schedule, the school day, or the school calendar.

Building time for professional development into the regular school day conveys a message about the importance of continuous and ongoing learning. Teachers will make an increased effort to participate in such offerings when they perceive the value attributed to the activities (DuFour et al., 2008). Furthermore, in high-performing schools, principals ensure teachers communicate regularly to remove barriers to student learning and to discuss effective teaching and learning strategies (NEA, 2008). It is important that the elementary school principal protects the use of this dedicated collaborative time in order to ensure teacher learning team tasks are accomplished as assigned.

Equity and Access

Teacher equity and access to professional development and learning experiences are a third design issue. The goal is to pursue high within-school teacher knowledge quality and low between-teacher implementation variance in terms of mathematics content and pedagogical knowledge. As Barber and Mourshed (2007) report in *How the World's Best Performing School Systems Come Out on Top*, the world's highest-performing school systems are able to "decrease the pedagogical variability between teachers and increase the quality of instruction . . . they do this by establishing clear instructional priorities and investing in teacher preparation and professional development" (p. 12).

It is important, then, that all teachers and mathematics specialists have access to the district's or school's ongoing professional development and are required to fully engage and participate in the professional learning community team for professional development established by the school or district. The principal should also expect the teachers and mathematics specialists to act on the professional development content to ensure the experience includes issues of equitable opportunities for all students to learn relevant and meaningful mathematics.

Loucks-Horsley and colleagues (2003) suggest several critical questions for the principal to consider when building coherence, focus, and fairness into the professional development opportunities for teacher learning teams. The following feature box provides an adaptation of their suggestions.

Ensuring Professional Development Equity for All Teachers

1. Is access to the professional development opportunities available to all, or does it favor adults in certain locations, grade levels, or from different cultural groups?

2. Does the design of the professional development ensure full engagement and learning by the participants?

3. Does the mathematical content of the professional development experience include the issues of equitable opportunity to learn for all students?

4. Does the mathematical content of the professional development experience include an active response to students who are struggling to learn?

5. Does the professional development emphasize teaching new content and concepts in ways that align with the eight CCSS Mathematical Practices?

6. Does the professional development emphasize assessing mathematical content and concepts in ways that provide immediate and corrective feedback and also promote both teacher and student self-reflection on learning progress?

Source: Adapted from Loucks-Horsley et al., 2003.

Ultimately, the professional development question for the elementary school principal is not as much about the provision of time as it is about how the principal will ensure the most effective use of the time dedicated to the teacher learning team for professional development. This distinction requires the principal to have a well-focused professional development plan for the content work of the collaborative teacher learning teams.

Three Content Agreements for Designing Professional Development in Mathematics

In order to build teacher knowledge capacity and sustain implementation of that knowledge into the classroom, the professional development content should be framed around three critical agreements: (1) what to learn, (2) how to assess what to learn, and (3) how to respond.

What to Learn

The first question for implementing professional development is, What do we want students to learn at each grade level or in each course? This question, more specifically, addresses the mathematical knowledge, skills, understandings, and dispositions that students are expected to acquire as a result of each unit of mathematics instruction. A school committed to helping all students learn must ensure that the professional development provides great clarity and low teacher-to-teacher variance on this question.

Determining how to implement the *what* is one of the primary tasks of every grade-level or course-based teacher team. The following feature box highlights questions every elementary school principal should ask in order to keep teacher teams focused on obtaining agreement and on implementing answers that will improve student learning. The very nature of the CCSS and the curriculum and instruction practices described in chapters 1 and 2 will dictate much of the response for the question about what students should learn at each grade level. However, the grade- or course-level team must attain crystal-clear agreement for daily implementation of the CCSS instructional vision. This represents the real work of the teacher teams.

Professional Development Work for Grade-Level Teacher Teams

1. Do we have clear agreement on what all students need to learn at each grade level or in each course?

2. What kinds of instruction will facilitate that learning for each unit of mathematics content?

3. What do and should our classrooms look like? Where are the gaps between our vision for mathematics instruction and the reality of our instruction?

4. How will we ensure the use of engaging learning opportunities for our students and meet the spirit of the CCSS Mathematical Practices?

5. What is our vision for teacher learning and sharing together?

6. How will our grade-level teams know which students are achieving intended learning goals? Based on what measures of learning? What common grade-level assessments?

---

continued →

7. What targets for improved student performance will the teacher learning team set?

8. How will we know students have gained expected grade-level knowledge and that we have met our learning targets?

9. How will we reflect on our teaching and learning and share that experience with one another?

10. How will we share our best models of high-quality mathematics teaching and learning?

The movement toward the CCSS will shift the agreement on what is to be learned for every grade level toward the "less is more" direction as fewer mathematics standards will be required at each grade. The caveat, however, is that teaching those required standards with greater depth for meaning and understanding will place great demands on the professional development work of your grade-level teacher teams.

How to Assess What to Learn

The second area of agreement centers on how to know if each student is learning the essential mathematics skills, concepts, understandings, and dispositions deemed most essential. This question reveals the greatest variability in quality teacher practice and acts as the linchpin in the professional development of mathematics teachers. In order for teachers and teacher teams to answer these questions, they should clarify what students must learn, and they must participate in the alignment of local unit assessments to district, state, or provincial standards. They should also develop common assessments and scoring rubrics that accurately reflect what students know in order to optimize student learning opportunities.

To adequately answer the "how do we know" question with fidelity, teacher teams pursue agreement on test items and work interdependently to decrease the wide variability in the quality, depth, and rigor of assessment instruments used across grade levels and courses. Professional development in mathematics should provide the necessary time, mentoring, and leadership necessary for mathematics teachers to analyze and reflect on student learning and data. Teacher collaboration is essential for achieving assessment excellence and for closing the equity gap. In *Challenges and Choices: The Role of Educational Leaders in Effective Assessment*, Reeves (2007) indicates that when assessment results and data are examined a few times a week as part of an ongoing professional development practice, chances of becoming a gap-closing school significantly increase.

How to Respond

The third critical area of agreement outlines the intentional response when some students do not learn and how quickly this response will occur. The vertical nature of the mathematics curriculum and the interconnectedness of content learning arcs require an efficient and formative response by students and teachers immediately following hourly, daily, weekly, or unit-by-unit demonstrations of a student's lack of understanding. This understanding, or lack thereof, pertains specifically to the expected outcomes for all learners. Professional development that supports the work of teacher teams in the use of formative assessment facilitates effective teacher dialogue. It also promotes interdependent practice of ongoing student feedback for student learning. This includes teacher reflection for lesson redesign.

The PRIME Leadership Framework (NCSM, 2008b) states that the purpose of assessment moves far beyond mere after-the-fact testing and should become an integral component of the planning-teaching-assessing cycle that characterizes high-quality instruction. To adequately respond to this issue, teachers and teacher teams must decide how to move forward each hour, day, week, or unit of study.

The teachers, as a team, must decide what to reteach and how to reteach it. They must also decide how to intervene; what required interventions to develop in class and outside of class to support student learning; how to address the needs of ELs, such as effective comprehension strategies; and how to adjust lesson plans and design meaningful instructional support to struggling students.

This is the real work of teacher learning teams. The professional development of mathematics teachers must help each teacher and each mathematics specialist make these decisions in the context of their workplace on an ongoing basis.

Priorities for Charting Improvement in Mathematics Professional Development

As you design and implement a professional development program in mathematics for faculty, consider the following questions, all in the context of the ongoing work of the teacher learning teams. Your answers to these questions will help identify the strengths of your current professional development program and the areas in which you may need to focus or redirect attention.

- Does the professional development help faculty members understand the importance of their individual and collective growth as an effect on increased achievement for all students in mathematics?

- Does the professional development increase grade-level mathematics achievement for all student groups?

- Does the professional development support implementation of the mathematics standards of the CCSS at the national, state, and local levels?

- Does professional development support the alignment of the curriculum, instruction, student assessment, and grade-level response to student assessment results in mathematics?

Too often, mathematics knowledge and skill development is focused on reading and language arts, but elementary and middle school teachers also need opportunities to continuously update their content knowledge skills in mathematics. Communicate to staff that mathematics learning is ongoing, every year, and sustained by collaborating with grade-level (grades K–5) or course-based (often the case in grades 6–8) teachers to identify new mathematics professional development goals in teams. Make time each year to provide ongoing feedback on mathematics learning-goal progress, and allow the teams to have a voice in setting those learning goals. As you communicate that teachers' mathematics professional development is an important ongoing supported process in the school, increased student achievement in mathematics will follow.

The elementary school cannot function successfully, however, without a clear plan for community involvement. The shifts in CCSS mathematics content and instruction will require the support and understanding of the families within the school community. Chapter 7 provides deep insight into how to do so effectively.

SEVEN
WORKING WITH FAMILIES

Families are their children's first teachers and are in prime position to have an important influence on their children's academic development. Through the values they communicate about education, effort, persistence, and responsibility, parents influence their children's mathematics achievement.

A meta-analysis of seventy-seven studies involving approximately 300,000 students found a positive relationship between amount and type of family involvement and student achievement (Jeynes, 2005): "The academic advantage for [students whose] parents were highly involved in their education averaged about 0.5–0.6 of a standard deviation for overall educational outcomes, grades, and academic achievement" (p. 2). Specifically, parental expectations, parenting style, reading to children, and participation in school-related activities influenced students' achievement, with parental expectations being particularly important. These results held for minority and low-income students as well as for the population in general.

In addition, families who are actively involved in their child's education report having a better relationship with their child's school and a higher satisfaction with the level of education their child is receiving. With respect to mathematics, Kober (1991) asserts that parental attitude toward mathematics is a good predictor of children's mathematics achievement at all grade levels. She cites research showing that "children's self-concept and confidence in their own mathematics aptitude is more directly related to their parents' perceptions of their competence than to children's own achievement record" (p. 47). In addition,

> Given this reality, it is crucial for schools to form strong relationships with families. Students benefit when you and your teachers work together to encourage parents to: create a home environment that encourages learning; express high (but realistic) expectations for their children's achievement and future careers; and become involved in their children's education at school and in the community. (School-Home Links, 2001, p. 2)

This chapter explores ways in which schools and families can collaborate to promote mathematics achievement, and it identifies resources to help you and your teachers work with your families to support their children's education. In addition, the chapter includes activities that can be done at home to reinforce mathematical concepts.

The Diversity of Families

Families have a variety of structures. Only 67 percent of children under the age of eighteen live with two married parents; this includes families with stepparents. Mother-only families comprise 23 percent, and 4 percent of kids live in father-only families. About 4 percent of children live without either parent. These percentages differ significantly for African American and Hispanic children compared to non-Hispanic white children. According to the Federal Interagency Forum on Child and Family Statistics (2009), "In 2008, 35 percent of black children and 64 percent of Hispanic children lived with two married parents, compared with 75 percent of non-Hispanic white children under age 18" (p. 1). Furthermore, only 25 percent of families with children under eighteen fit the traditional "two parents, one employed" model. Instead, both parents are employed in 44 percent of families, and 21 percent of families have a single, employed parent. In 10 percent of families, the parents are unemployed. While family structure does not determine how much parents care about their children's education, it does influence the amount of time parents might have to be actively involved in their children's education.

In general, the term *family* here refers to any family configuration, and *parents* include a child's primary caregiver, whether or not the parent is a biological relative, step-, or adoptive parent.

Approaches to Encourage Family Engagement

Parents need basic information about their child's mathematics class—copies of course outlines, assignments, and other materials that may assist them in understanding their child's mathematics program. They also need much more than that, as illustrated in the following vignette from a parent math night.

> Ames Elementary School scheduled its first parent math night in November. As the evening's presentation starts, a man in his early thirties in a Pittsburgh Penguins' ski jacket raises his hand and says in exasperation. "So, what is with this math program? Every night after dinner, I sit down with my son Tommy to help him with his homework. Every night, we fight about math! I tell him, you have to start adding from the right; he says, 'No, you don't. That's not the way we do it. I can start adding at the left—or anywhere.' So, then I say, 'No, that's not how you do it.' But Tommy gets the right answers—and explains to me what he's doing. Is that OK? I'm very frustrated!"

This father is trying to support his child's mathematics learning—helping with homework on a regular basis, communicating the importance of learning math, and coming to a parent night—things we would like all parents to do. He was also doing what he thought were the right things to support his son, based on *his* school experience. Parents who care about learning often help their children with math homework; that is, they show their children the steps to solve problems. What the father needed, however, was an understanding of what mathematics curriculum and instruction looks like today and specific suggestions about ways to help his child other than showing him the steps in a procedure.

There are three specific areas in which you can provide more information to help support effective parental involvement: (1) provide descriptions of mathematics curriculum and instruction in their child's classroom, (2) provide specific ways parents can help their children, and (3) provide specific information to support and promote preschool success.

Provide Descriptions of Mathematics Instruction in Their Children's Classroom

First and foremost, provide families an accurate and detailed description of how mathematics instruction looks in their child's classroom, with special attention to the aspects most different from what they likely experienced as students or with their older children. The aspects of the CCSS identified in chapter 1 most different for teachers will certainly be different for parents too, such as the Mathematical Practices "instruction that starts with solving a wide variety of problems" and "developing and justifying informal computational procedures in the early grades" with proficiency in standard algorithms delayed until grades 4, 5, or 6.

The following feature box summarizes classroom features to highlight with parents.

How Will Mathematics Look in Your Child's Classroom?

As a result of efforts to strengthen the mathematics curricula and ensure children are prepared for college or careers, the instruction you can expect in your child's mathematics classes may look quite different from what you experienced when you were in elementary school.

For instance, in effective math classrooms today, you will see the following:

Children are expected to know both basic arithmetic skills and the mathematical concepts that are the basis of these skills—Children are learning and applying basic computational skills, and they will also be learning about the properties of operations and relationships in our number system so that they understand why computational procedures work.

Children are using computation strategies and alternate algorithms before learning standard algorithms (procedures)—Children create informal ways to solve computation problems using properties of operations and knowledge of our base-ten number system. They are also using a variety of algorithms before learning more standard procedures for adding, subtracting, multiplying, and dividing multidigit numbers.

Children are doing more than arithmetic—Children see that mathematics is much more than arithmetic (knowing the facts and number operations); it involves estimation, mental-math geometry, measurement, data, and more.

Children are striving to achieve high standards and are assessed regularly to determine their progress—Children will be achieving high standards of understanding, complexity, and accuracy set for them by their parents, teachers, schools, and states or provinces.

---

continued →

Children are solving challenging problems to learn new mathematical ideas, concepts, and skills—Children perform challenging tasks designed to help them investigate new ideas. They talk and write explanations for their thinking.

Children are working with one another—Children sometimes collaborate to make discoveries, draw conclusions, and discuss mathematical concepts and operations.

Children are evaluated in a variety of ways—Teachers use many different ways to determine if children know and understand mathematical concepts. Some of these ways include open-ended questions in which a student writes out the steps—or thought processes—used in solving a math problem, independent and group projects, and other written tests.

Children are learning to use calculators appropriately—Children are using calculators not as crutches, but as tools for performing operations with large numbers. Use of a calculator will not replace a thorough knowledge of basic mathematical operations.

Children are using computers appropriately—Children are using computers to run software that poses unique and interesting problem situations that would not be available to them without the technology.

Source: Adapted from Carnine & Lehr, 2005; Kanter & Darby, 1999.

To introduce these features, it is helpful to highlight research about how people learn in general, as well as how they learn mathematics (see chapter 2). It is also important for parents to understand there is a research-informed rationale for the instructional changes in your school. As much as possible, relate these features to parents' prior, perhaps informal, knowledge. For example, you might ask parents to do some mental computation (for instance, find 29×12, $81 - 27$, and so forth) to introduce the idea of alternate algorithms.

You also need to be cognizant of parents' concerns and address these issues; this will engage parents as allies, rather than opponents, to the changes in mathematics instruction. According to research from the Public Agenda Foundation (1993), parents want their children to become problem solvers and mathematical thinkers. First, though, they want their children to know the basics—number facts and computational procedures (Briars, 1999). Thus when emphasizing conceptual understanding and the CCSS Mathematical Practices, don't overlook or understate the basics that parents value.

Finally, provide information about assessments as well as curriculum and instruction. While parents may remember taking multiple-choice tests, they may be unfamiliar with newer performance assessments, especially those being developed for CCSS. One strategy to introduce parents to new assessment types is to host a Take the Test Night, where parents take sample multiple-choice and performance assessments (under realistic timed conditions, of course), then score their own assessments. Parents at such an event are surprised at the level of some of the questions, and come away with a better understanding of why performance assessments are important (Briars, 1999).

Provide Specific Ways Parents Can Help Their Children

Most parents want to help their children learn mathematics. As the vignette illustrates, traditional ways of helping, such as showing children the steps to get answers, are not usually applicable to today's mathematics, which emphasizes students solving high-level tasks and developing conceptual understanding, thinking, and reasoning. Parents need specific suggestions and directions about productive ways to help their children. The following feature box contains some basic suggestions.

How Parents Can Help Their Children Learn Mathematics

Parents can engage in the following activities with their children to support mathematics instruction and learning.

Memorizing basic facts—Although it is important that children learn the meaning underlying basic addition, subtraction, multiplication, and division facts first, it is ultimately important for children to develop immediate fact recall. Immediate recall is a function of practice—and there is limited time in the school day for such practice. Basic fact practice can be a parental responsibility. Note that this practice does not require any materials—orally presenting facts promotes immediate recall better than worksheets. Perfect times to practice are while driving, walking, waiting, and so on.

Games—Games are a great way to practice mathematics concepts and skills, and they also promote positive parent-child relationships. One simple game is Top-It or Beat-It. All the cards from a math card deck are dealt to the players (to make a math deck from a regular deck of cards, use a marker to make the queens 0s, the aces 1s, and then number the kings and jacks 11 through 20). Players each keep the cards in a pile, face down. Each player turns up the top card; highest card wins. This basic number comparison game is good for young children. The game also provides basic fact practice for older children if each player turns over two cards and the comparison is the largest sum, difference, or product.

Problem solving—Because students will be working on complex problems at home, parents need strategies for how to help their children without solving the problems for them. Provide parents with a list of appropriate questions. These may include:

- What are you being asked to find out?
- What does the problem tell you?
- Can you tell me the problem in your own words?
- Is there anything that you don't understand? Where can you find answers to your questions?
- What will you try first? Next?
- Will it help to draw a picture? Act it out? Make a list?
- How do you know if your answer is right or wrong?
- What do you estimate the answer will be?
- Have you ever worked a problem like this before?

Mathematics everywhere—Mathematics problems are part of everyday life. Encourage parents to engage their children in solving everyday problems as they arise. *Helping Your Child Learn Mathematics* (U.S. Department of Education, 2004) has many suggestions for such problems.

Source: Adapted from Math & Science Collaborative, 2005.

Provide Specific Information to Support and Promote Preschool Success

A meta-analysis of six longitudinal studies found that children's understanding of mathematics concepts when they enter kindergarten is the most powerful predictor of later school success (Duncan et al., 2007). Thus it is important to also provide suggestions for how parents can support their preschoolers' learning of mathematics.

Helping Your Child Learn Math (Carnine & Lehr, 2005) contains suggestions for preschoolers as well as older children. In addition, Ramani and Siegler (2008) have found that home experience playing number board games, such as Chutes and Ladders, correlated positively with children's early numerical knowledge. They also found that low-income preschoolers were less likely to play board games at home than middle-income students; however, when low-income students had the opportunity to play simple-number board games, their proficiency in numeral identification, counting, and comparing numbers increased. Encouraging parents to play board games with their preschool children can have important payoffs for their mathematics learning.

Finally, in working with families, talk about parents' own dispositions toward mathematics and the influence parents can have on their children's attitudes and performance. Parents who communicate "Math is hard" or "It's OK that you're not doing well in math. I never did well, either" promote attitudes that are counterproductive for their children's success. Instead, they should give messages consistent with Dweck's (2007) work on growth mindsets: success in mathematics comes from hard work and effort, it's something that everyone can do, and it's important to do well in mathematics to be prepared for your future.

Engaging Families in Mathematics Activities

There are a variety of ways to engage families in mathematics. This section includes details on some of the most common practices, including math nights, family math sessions, parent-teacher conferences, and more.

Math Nights

Sponsoring math nights—informational or training sessions for parents on mathematics—is one way to facilitate home-school communication. During these sessions, parents engage in activities they can do with their children and learn about the mathematics program. This is also an opportunity for teachers to communicate their expectations for students. Parents need to know the standards to which students will be held and the expectations for their child's development over the course of the school year. Similarly, teachers should be certain to explicitly explain procedures for homework and borrowing manipulative materials, as well as expectations for special projects to make familial involvement in these activities as easy as possible.

Family Math Sessions

A variation on math night is to invite children to come with their parents to do math together. The benefits of this are that children get to explain how they do math to their parents and learn activities and games that they can do at home together.

As you plan math nights or family math sessions, remember that your school is not necessarily the best place for these events. Some parents have negative attitudes about mathematics or about school in general and are very intimidated by the thought of coming into a school. Others may have transportation or child-care issues. Sometimes, other venues, such as community centers and churches, are more conducive to a positive experience for parents around mathematics.

Back-to-School Nights, Parent-Teacher Conferences, and Parent Volunteers

Back-to-school nights and parent-teacher conferences provide another forum for conveying information on the mathematics program. Back-to-school night serves as an ideal opportunity for teachers to give parents a tour of the room and its mathematical materials and to explain the mathematics program. During conferences, teachers can show parents examples of their child's work, results of assessment measures (such as observational notes or tests), and the activities in which their child has participated in class.

You can also encourage parents who have extra time to volunteer in classrooms. Being a "math mom" or "math dad" is a wonderful way for parents to understand the mathematics program and learn how to support their child, as well as other children.

Math Newsletters

Sending home a weekly or monthly newsletter is another way to keep parents informed. At the beginning of the year, the newsletter might contain a timeline of the development of mathematical concepts and skills students are expected to master by the end of each academic quarter. Teachers can also include tips for helping children with their homework, instructions for games to support student learning, and other information on class activities, special projects, and upcoming events.

The Wisconsin Center for Education Research has developed the *Mathematics for Parents Newsletter* to assist teachers in communicating with parents about how children learn mathematics. Each newsletter addresses one mathematical concept or skill and explains how it develops, common misconceptions that surround it, and good practices to support its development. The newsletters are sent home with students as new concepts or skills are introduced during the course of the year. Visit www.wcer.wisc.edu/archive/mims/Parent_Newsletters/ for online versions of the newsletters.

Priorities for Charting Improvement in Family Engagement

There are student learning benefits to a strong family engagement program. Yet recognizing its importance does not always translate to implementation, commitment, and resource allocation. To make this happen, you and your grade-level teacher teams must make strong family-school partnership support a priority. When you make it clear that family involvement is important, teachers and teacher teams are more likely to use family engagement strategies.

Moreover, for family engagement efforts to be successful, they must be a school priority. Transforming a school into an institution that treats families as partners in the students' education will take time, and the effort will not always go smoothly. Unintended consequences are bound to occur, including personality conflicts between parents and groups who do not fully understand legal and district restrictions or boundaries on parent behavior. As you lead family involvement efforts in the school, you will need to monitor and nurture the effort continuously.

Above all, as principal, you and your faculty possess the primary responsibility for initiating school-family partnerships. Professional development that supports family engagement, creating time for staff to work with parents, supplying necessary resources, designing innovative strategies to meet the needs of diverse families, and providing useful information to families on how they can contribute to their children's learning is well worth the effort (Funkhouser & Gonzales, 1997).

The following feature box, a section adapted from the U.S. Department of Education's *Partnership for Family Involvement in Education* (1998), provides specific ideas for enhancing family involvement and support.

Partners in Learning: How Schools Can Support Family Involvement in Education

Principals can increase family involvement with the following endeavors.

Learn to communicate better—At times, parents feel that educators talk down to them or speak in educational jargon they do not understand. School signs often seem unwelcoming. Schools should make every effort to reach out and communicate with parents in a clear way and listen to what they have to say. To ensure all parents have access to information, written material should be concise and easily readable. Schools should be parent friendly. Some school newsletters for parents might include a glossary of terms to help parents understand school improvement efforts. Other schools use regularly scheduled telephone calls to stay in contact with families.

Encourage parental participation in school improvement efforts—When schools develop improvement plans, families should be included at every stage of the process to attain their input and to offer them a sense of shared responsibility. Because of NCLB, many schools are now developing such plans; they are working to raise academic standards, improve teaching, make schools safer, introduce computers and other learning technologies into the classroom, and make many other vitally needed changes. The full involvement of parents and other members of the community is instrumental to the success of these efforts.

Involve parents in decision making—Schools can give parents a more effective voice by opening up the school governance process so that more parents can participate. Many schools hold evening and weekend meetings and conferences to accommodate families' work schedules.

Give teachers the tools to reach out to families—Professional development can help teachers understand the benefits of family engagement and show them how to remove barriers to engagement. It can also explain techniques for improving two-way communication between home and schools and suggest ways to help meet families' overall educational needs.

Make parents feel welcome—Often, the first time a parent comes to school is when a child is in trouble. Schools can help reduce tensions by making initial contacts with parents friendly and respectful. Schools can also reduce distrust by arranging contacts in neutral settings off school grounds. Home visits by family liaison personnel can be particularly helpful. Some programs have used home-school coordinators to run weekly clubs for parents, helping build parenting skills and trust. Schools might also encourage parents, teachers, and students to meet at the beginning of the school year to agree on goals and develop a common understanding.

Overcome language barriers—Reaching families whose first language is not English requires schools to make special accommodations. Translating materials into a parent's first language helps, but written communication alone is not enough. Ideally, a resource person, perhaps another parent, should be available to communicate with parents in their first language. Interactive telephone voicemail systems that have bilingual recordings for families are also useful. In addition, English-as-a-second-language classes for parents and grandparents may be helpful.

Use technology to link parents to the classroom—The Internet makes it possible to communicate with families in new ways. School and district webpages provide places to post mathematics resources as well as specific information about the mathematics program and activities. Schools are increasingly using sites like www.mygradebook.com to enable parents to monitor their children's progress. While the Internet has great potential as a communications tool, it is important to keep in mind families who do not have access to these resources and to provide them with information via more traditional means.

Encourage communities to join school-family partnerships—Partnerships can be especially effective in reducing a school's safety problems connected to problems in surrounding neighborhoods. Parents, community residents, and law enforcement officials can help by joining together in voluntary organizations, friendship networks, and neighborhood watches to solve common problems. Schools and community and religious organizations can help by offering after-school cultural and recreational activities. Community-supported student services have also succeeded when families, schools, and community representatives have made the effort to get involved.

EIGHT
TURNING THE MATHEMATICS VISION INTO ACTION

The Common Core State Standards and the accountability of the Elementary and Secondary Education Act will have a continued and dramatic impact on all levels of K–8 student performance in mathematics. The expected vision and outcomes for student learning in mathematics will only continue to exceed current levels of school performance. In schools and classrooms across the country, educators are working to improve the access and achievement of all students in mathematics. National and international assessments of students' mathematics knowledge have revealed that K–8 U.S. students are improving but not at the same rate as many of their international counterparts (Haycock, 2009). U.S. student performance and access to college and career readiness opportunities continue to highlight significant gaps among minority students (Haycock, 2011).

Goldsmith (2001) explains "as instructional leaders of their schools, principals can contribute to efforts to improve mathematics education in three important ways: (1) becoming knowledgeable about the goals and strategies of mathematics education reform, (2) guiding and supporting school improvement efforts, and (3) involving parents and community members" (p. 53). Additionally, principals need to set a tone of high expectations for all students and encourage teachers to use instructional strategies that promote the development of "active and independent mathematical thinkers" (p. 53).

In order to improve students' mathematical achievement, elementary school leaders must change the mathematics that students learn, and the ways in which they learn it, to meet the vision described in this book, as well as the Common Core State Standards. The new mathematics curriculum emphasizes conceptual understanding, problem-solving skills, procedural skill mastery, and competence in communicating mathematical ideas, as well as the development and demonstration of higher-order thinking. The CCSS Mathematical Practices no longer leave this type of teacher lesson planning and assessment design to chance—it is now required.

Developing a mathematics program and a school culture that better meet the needs of *all* students in your school begins with providing teachers ongoing daily and weekly professional development and learning. This occurs as part of a grade-level or course-based learning team dedicated to information on high-quality, effective mathematics instruction.

The development of an effective mathematics program requires horizontal and vertical curriculum alignment to the CCSS and the learning progressions of content described in chapter 1. Principals must also be intentional about lesson design elements that create greater student understanding, ongoing formative assessment cycles for adult and student learning, additional and intentional RTI assistance, and faculty and staff content-level professional development. If not already doing so, principals should seriously consider using an elementary mathematics specialist or coach to support these goals and expectations.

A key part of this process will be the ability to bring *coherence* to all the pieces from a district or schoolwide perspective by answering these questions:

- Is your approach to mathematics instruction balanced and research affirmed? Has it been effectively communicated to all staff so that the intended curriculum is actually the implemented curriculum at all grade levels? How do you know this to be true?

- Are the curriculum and instructional strategies for developing conceptual understanding within the content domains of the CCSS well integrated and cohesive across the grades with full understanding of the CCSS Mathematical Practices?

- Are you providing sufficient instructional time in class for students to learn mathematics?

- Do you have a comprehensive and ongoing approach to RTI that identifies students struggling in mathematics and targets specific mathematical learning challenges—an approach that ensures no student will be overlooked by the classroom teacher with little chance of catching up to the pace of the curriculum?

- Does your RTI system provide intensive support for struggling students and use a variety of venues (tutoring, after-school sessions, regrouping by mathematics ability, and so forth) with supportive mathematics instruction time for these students?

- Are professional development and learning supports available for teachers so they can use assessment data to both guide instruction and understand how to teach and reteach specific concepts and procedural knowledge and skills?

- Do you provide adequate and protected time for teachers to collaborate to solve problems, share successful approaches, and discuss how to provide assistance for students struggling in mathematics?

As the school leader, supporting the efforts of all teachers to promote students' mathematics skills is essential. As principal, you can help by providing resources and time for teachers to build their skills, discuss what works, and collaborate in a schoolwide effort to increase the ability of all students to achieve mathematics with success. Principals set the tone by modeling enthusiasm for mathematics, participating in mathematics discussions alongside the grade-level or course-based teacher teams, encouraging staff to use new ways of working with struggling students, communicating with parents, and demonstrating a positive disposition and love of mathematics to each student.

To be a successful principal, implementing the vision of the CCSS and the expectations described in this book must become a shared and owned process by all stakeholders. Distributed ownership of the focused effort on improved mathematics results and commitment to the right things is one of your primary responsibilities.

The following steps enable this accomplishment:

1. Create a process for focused implementation on all elements of the CCSS vision.

2. Build in accountability to the CCSS implementation as part of the "way we do work around here," rather than a random act of the leader passing judgment on others.

3. Build in celebration as a critical element of positive consequences to teacher team work of the CCSS. The "How did we do?" aspect of making progress toward goals will turn your vision for mathematics into reality as it does the following:

   a. Designs measurable outcomes and results

   b. Connects vision to any level of strategic planning

   c. Requires that adults focus risk taking and action on the CCSS

If it is not already in place, develop an intentional celebration plan, as soon as possible, that connects to an improvement cycle for student learning at each grade level. Reflect on how you and the faculty are making progress in turning the vision described in this book into action.

Make celebration an intentional part of your leadership life. Begin publicly and privately celebrating now. Celebrate results; and more important, celebrate adult actions that reflect the passionate pursuit of the teaching and learning of mathematics. Don't delay. Don't make excuses. Don't say you are too busy to notice what is happening with the mathematics program in your school. Be intentional and build a teaching and learning community with those on your staff. Help staff better understand the transformed expectations for teaching mathematics in the new age of the CCSS. Then enjoy the transformation of improved student achievement in your school.

APPENDIX A
CCSS STANDARDS FOR MATHEMATICAL PRACTICE

Source: CCSSO, 2010a, pp. 6–8. Used with permission.

The Standards for Mathematical Practice describe varieties of expertise that mathematics educators at all levels should seek to develop in their students. These practices rest on important "processes and proficiencies" with longstanding importance in mathematics education. The first of these are the NCTM process standards of problem solving, reasoning and proof, communication, representation, and connections. The second are the strands of mathematical proficiency specified in the National Research Council's report *Adding It Up*: adaptive reasoning, strategic competence, conceptual understanding (comprehension of mathematical concepts, operations and relations), procedural fluency (skill in carrying out procedures flexibly, accurately, efficiently and appropriately), and productive disposition (habitual inclination to see mathematics as sensible, useful, and worthwhile, coupled with a belief in diligence and one's own efficacy).

1. Make sense of problems and persevere in solving them.

Mathematically proficient students start by explaining to themselves the meaning of a problem and looking for entry points to its solution. They analyze givens, constraints, relationships, and goals. They make conjectures about the form and meaning of the solution and plan a solution pathway rather than simply jumping into a solution attempt. They consider analogous problems, and try special cases and simpler forms of the original problem in order to gain insight into its solution. They monitor and evaluate their progress and change course if necessary. Older students might, depending on the context of the problem, transform algebraic expressions or change the viewing window on their graphing calculator to get the information they need. Mathematically proficient students can explain correspondences between equations, verbal descriptions, tables, and graphs or draw diagrams of important features and relationships, graph data, and search for regularity or trends. Younger students might rely on using concrete objects or pictures to help conceptualize and solve a problem. Mathematically proficient students check their answers to problems using a different method, and they continually ask themselves, "Does this make sense?" They can understand the approaches of others to solving complex problems and identify correspondences between different approaches.

2. Reason abstractly and quantitatively.

Mathematically proficient students make sense of quantities and their relationships in problem situations. They bring two complementary abilities to bear on problems involving quantitative relationships: the ability to *decontextualize*—to abstract a given situation and represent it symbolically and manipulate the representing symbols as if they have a life of their own, without necessarily attending to their referents—and the ability to contextualize, to pause as needed during the manipulation process in order to probe into the referents for the symbols involved. Quantitative reasoning entails habits of creating a coherent representation of the problem at hand; considering the units involved; attending to the meaning of quantities, not just how to compute them; and knowing and flexibly using different properties of operations and objects.

3. Construct viable arguments and critique the reasoning of others.

Mathematically proficient students understand and use stated assumptions, definitions, and previously established results in constructing arguments. They make conjectures and build a logical progression of statements to explore the truth of their conjectures. They are able to analyze situations by breaking them into cases, and can recognize and use counterexamples. They justify their conclusions, communicate them to others, and respond to the arguments of others. They reason inductively about data, making plausible arguments that take into account the context from which the data arose. Mathematically proficient students are also able to compare the effectiveness of two plausible arguments, distinguish correct logic or reasoning from that which is flawed, and—if there is a flaw in an argument—explain what it is. Elementary students can construct arguments using concrete referents such as objects, drawings, diagrams, and actions. Such arguments can make sense and be correct, even though they are not generalized or made formal until later grades. Later, students learn to determine domains to which an argument applies. Students at all grades can listen to or read the arguments of others, decide whether they make sense, and ask useful questions to clarify or improve the arguments.

4. Model with mathematics.

Mathematically proficient students can apply the mathematics they know to solve problems arising in everyday life, society, and the workplace. In early grades, this might be as simple as writing an addition equation to describe a situation. In middle grades, a student might apply proportional reasoning to plan a school event or analyze a problem in the community. By high school, a student might use geometry to solve a design problem or use a function to describe how one quantity of interest depends on another. Mathematically proficient students who can apply what they know are comfortable making assumptions and approximations to simplify a complicated situation, realizing that these may need revision later. They are able to identify important quantities in a practical situation and map their relationships using such tools as diagrams, two-way tables, graphs, flowcharts and formulas. They can analyze those relationships mathematically to draw conclusions. They routinely interpret their mathematical results in the context of the situation and reflect on whether the results make sense, possibly improving the model if it has not served its purpose.

5. Use appropriate tools strategically.

Mathematically proficient students consider the available tools when solving a mathematical problem. These tools might include pencil and paper, concrete models, a ruler, a protractor, a calculator, a spreadsheet, a computer algebra system, a statistical package, or dynamic geometry software. Proficient students are sufficiently familiar with tools appropriate for their grade or course to make sound decisions about when each of these tools might be helpful, recognizing both the insight to be gained and their limitations. For example, mathematically proficient high school students analyze graphs of functions and solutions generated using a graphing calculator. They detect possible errors by strategically using estimation and other mathematical knowledge. When making mathematical models, they know that technology can enable them to visualize the results of varying assumptions, explore consequences, and compare predictions with data. Mathematically proficient students at various grade levels are able to identify relevant external mathematical resources, such as digital content located on a website, and use them to pose or solve problems. They are able to use technological tools to explore and deepen their understanding of concepts.

6. Attend to precision.

Mathematically proficient students try to communicate precisely to others. They try to use clear definitions in discussion with others and in their own reasoning. They state the meaning of the symbols they choose, including using the equal sign consistently and appropriately. They are careful about specifying units of measure, and labeling axes to clarify the correspondence with quantities in a problem. They calculate accurately and efficiently, express numerical answers with a degree of precision appropriate for the problem context. In the elementary grades, students give carefully formulated explanations to each other. By the time they reach high school they have learned to examine claims and make explicit use of definitions.

7. Look for and make use of structure.

Mathematically proficient students look closely to discern a pattern or structure. Young students, for example, might notice that three and seven more is the same amount as seven and three more, or they may sort a collection of shapes according to how many sides the shapes have. Later, students will see 7×8 equals the well-remembered $7 \times 5 + 7 \times 3$, in preparation for learning about the distributive property. In the expression $x^2 + 9x + 14$, older students can see the 14 as 2×7 and the 9 as $2 + 7$. They recognize the significance of an existing line in a geometric figure and can use the strategy of drawing an auxiliary line for solving problems.

They also can step back for an overview and shift perspective. They can see complicated things, such as some algebraic expressions, as single objects or as being composed of several objects. For example, they can see $5 - 3(x - y)^2$ as 5 minus a positive number times a square and use that to realize that its value cannot be more than 5 for any real numbers x and y.

8. Look for and express regularity in repeated reasoning.

Mathematically proficient students notice if calculations are repeated, and look both for general methods and for shortcuts. Upper elementary students might notice when dividing 25 by 11 that they are repeating the same calculations over and over again, and conclude they have a repeating decimal. By paying attention to the calculation of slope as they repeatedly check whether points are on the line through $(1, 2)$ with slope 3, middle school students might abstract the equation $(y - 2)/(x - 1) = 3$. Noticing the regularity in the way terms cancel when expanding $(x - 1)(x + 1)$, $(x - 1)(x^2 + x + 1)$, and $(x - 1)(x^3 + x^2 + x + 1)$ might lead them to the general formula for the sum of a geometric series. As they work to solve a problem, mathematically proficient students maintain oversight of the process, while attending to the details. They continually evaluate the reasonableness of their intermediate results.

Connecting the Standards for Mathematical Practice to the Standards for Mathematical Content

The Standards for Mathematical Practice describe ways in which developing student practitioners of the discipline of mathematics increasingly ought to engage with the subject matter as they grow in mathematical maturity and expertise throughout the elementary, middle and high school years. Designers of curricula, assessments, and professional development should all attend to the need to connect the mathematical practices to mathematical content in mathematics instruction.

The Standards for Mathematical Content are a balanced combination of procedure and understanding. Expectations that begin with the word "understand" are often especially good opportunities to connect the practices to the content. Students who lack understanding of a topic may rely on procedures too heavily. Without a flexible base from which to work, they may be less likely to consider analogous problems, represent problems coherently, justify conclusions, apply the mathematics to practical situations, use technology mindfully to work with the mathematics, explain the mathematics accurately to other students, step back for an overview, or deviate from a known procedure to find a shortcut. In short, a lack of understanding effectively prevents a student from engaging in the mathematical practices.

In this respect, those content standards, which set an expectation of understanding, are potential "points of intersection" between the Standards for Mathematical Content and the Standards for Mathematical Practice. These points of intersection are intended to be weighted toward central and generative concepts in the school mathematics curriculum that most merit the time, resources, innovative energies, and focus necessary to qualitatively improve the curriculum, instruction, assessment, professional development, and student achievement in mathematics.

REFERENCES AND RESOURCES

Ainsworth, L. (2007). Common formative assessments: The centerpiece of an integrated standards-based assessment system. In D. Reeves (Ed.), *Ahead of the curve: The power of assessment to transform teaching and learning* (pp. 79–102). Bloomington, IN: Solution Tree Press.

Allensworth, E., Correa, M., & Ponisciak, S. (2008). *From high school to the future: ACT preparation—Too much, too, late* [Research report]. Chicago: Consortium on Chicago School Research.

Association of Mathematics Teacher Educators, Association of State Supervisors of Mathematics, National Council of Supervisors of Mathematics, & National Council of Teachers of Mathematics. (2010). *The role of elementary specialists in the teaching and learning of mathematics* [Joint position paper]. Accessed at www.mathedleadership.org/docs/resources/prime /JointStatementOnMathSpecialists.pdf on July 25, 2011.

Ball, D. L. (2010, April). *How can we get good teaching for all students?* Paper presented at the Scholastic Intervention Convention, Boca Raton, FL.

Barber, M., & Mourshed, M. (2007). *How the world's best performing school systems come out on top.* San Francisco: McKinsey & Company.

Bender, W. N., & Crane, D. (2011). *RTI in math: Practical guidelines for elementary teachers.* Bloomington, IN: Solution Tree Press.

Boaler, J., & Humphreys, C. (2005). *Connecting mathematical ideas: Middle school video cases to support teaching and learning.* Portsmouth, NH: Heinemann.

Bransford, J. D., Brown, A. L., & Cocking, T. (2000). *How people learn: Brain, mind, experience, and school* (Expanded ed.). Washington, DC: National Academies Press.

Bransford, J. D., & Donovan, M. S. (2005). Scientific inquiry and how people learn. In M. S. Donovan & J. D. Bransford (Eds.), *How students learn history, mathematics, and science* (pp. 397–419). Washington, DC: National Academies Press.

Bresser, R., Melanese, K., & Sphar, C. (2009). *Supporting English language learners in math class.* Sausalito, CA: Math Solutions.

Briars, D. J. (1999). A tactic for educating parents. *School Administrator, 56*(1), 34.

Campbell, P. F., & Malkus, N. N. (2011). The impact of elementary mathematics coaches on student achievement. *Elementary School Journal, 111*(3), 430–454.

Carnine, D., & Lehr, R. (2005). *Helping your child learn math.* Washington, DC: U.S. Department of Education. Accessed at www.ed.gov/pubs/parents/Math on July 25, 2011.

Charles, R. (Ed.). (2010). *Teaching and learning mathematics: Translating research for school administrators.* Reston, VA: National Council of Teachers of Mathematics.

Clark County School District. (n.d.). *Mathematics resources for your family* [Brochure]. Las Vegas, NV: Author. Accessed at www.ccsd.net/areas/2/pdf/Parent_Corner/MathParentBrochure.pdf on August 23, 2011.

Clements, D. H. (2007). Curriculum research: Toward a framework for research-based curricula. *Journal for Research in Mathematics Education, 38,* 35–70.

Clements, D. H., & Sarama, J. (2009). *Learning and teaching early math: The learning trajectories approach.* New York: Routledge.

Clements, D. H., Sarama, J., Spitler, M. E., Lange, A. A., & Wolfe, C. B. (2011). Mathematics learned by young children in an intervention based on learning trajectories: A large-scale cluster randomized trial. *Journal for Research in Mathematics Education, 42*(2), 127–166.

Conference Board of the Mathematical Sciences. (2001). *Mathematical education of teachers.* Washington, DC: Author.

Conference Board of the Mathematical Sciences. (in press). *Mathematical education of teachers.* Washington, DC: Author.

Confrey, J. (2008, July). *A synthesis of the research on rational number reasoning: A learning progressions approach to synthesis.* Paper presented at the 11th International Congress of Mathematics Instruction, Monterrey, Mexico.

Council of Chief State School Officers. (2010a). *Common core state standards.* Washington, DC: Author.

Council of Chief State School Officers. (2010b). *Model core teaching standards: A resource for state dialogue.* Washington, DC: Author.

Cross, C. T., Woods, T. A., & Schweingruber, H. (Eds.). (2009). *Mathematics learning in early childhood: Paths toward excellence and equity.* Washington, DC: National Academies Press.

Darling-Hammond, L., & Richardson, N. (2009). Teacher learning: What matters? *Educational Leadership, 66*(5), 46–53.

Donovan, M. S., & Bransford, J. D. (Eds.). (2005). *How students learn history, mathematics, and science.* Washington, DC: National Academies Press.

DuFour, R., DuFour, R., & Eaker, R. (2008). *Revisiting professional learning communities at work.* Bloomington, IN: Solution Tree Press.

Duncan, G. J., Dowsett, C. J., Claessens, A., Magnuson, K., Huston, A. C., Klebanov, P., et al. (2007). School readiness and later achievement. *Developmental Psychology, 43,* 1428–1446.

Dweck, C. S. (2007). The perils and promises of praise. *Educational Leadership, 65,* 34–39.

Ehrenberg, R. E., Brewer, D. J., Gamoran, A., & Willms, J. D. (2001). Does class size matter? *Scientific American, 285*(5), 78–85.

Federal Interagency Forum on Child and Family Statistics. (2009). *America's children: Key national indicators of well-being.* Accessed at www.childstats.gov/pdf/ac2009/ac_09.pdf on January 11, 2011.

Fennell, F. (2007). President's message: What's so special about special education? Everything! *NCTM News Bulletin.* Accessed at www.nctm.org/uploadedFiles/About_NCTM /President/2007_10PresMsg.pdf on July 26, 2011.

Fennell, F. (2010). *Focus math intensive intervention.* Glenview, IL: Pearson.

Fennell, F. (Ed.). (2011a). *Achieving fluency: Special education and mathematics.* Reston, VA: National Council of Teachers of Mathematics.

Fennell, F. (2011b). Elementary Mathematics Specialists and Teacher Leaders Project. Accessed at www2.mcdaniel.edu/emstl/index.html on July 25, 2011.

Franke, M. L., & Carey, D. A. (1996). Young children's perceptions of mathematics in problem solving environments. *Journal for Research in Mathematics Education, 28*(1), 8–25.

Franke, M. L., Kazemi, E., & Battery, D. (2007). Mathematics teaching and classroom practice. In F. K. Lester Jr. (Ed.), *Second handbook of research on mathematics teaching and learning* (pp. 255–256). Charlotte, NC: Information Age.

Fuchs, D., Fuchs, L. S., & Vaughn, S. (Eds.). (2008). *Response to intervention.* Newark, DE: International Reading Association.

Fuchs, L. S, Fuchs, D., Compton, D. L., Bryant, J. D., Hamlett, C. L., & Seethaler, P. (2007). Mathematics screening and progress monitoring at first grade: Implications for responsiveness to intervention. *Exceptional Children, 73*(3), 311–330.

Funkhouser, J. E., & Gonzales, M. R. (1997). *Family involvement in children's education—successful local approaches: An idea book.* Washington, DC: Government Printing Office.

Fuson, K. C., Kalchman, M., & Bransford, J. D. (2005). Mathematical understanding: An introduction. In S. Donovan & J. D. Bransford (Eds.), *How students learn: History, mathematics, and science in the classroom* (pp. 217–256). Washington, DC: National Academies Press.

Gersten, R., Baker, S., & Chard, D. (2006, November). *Effective instructional practices for students with difficulties in mathematics—findings from a research synthesis.* Paper presented at the Center on Instruction Mathematics Summit, Annapolis, MD.

Gersten, R., Beckmann, S., Clarke, B., Foegen, A., Marsh, L., Star, J. R., et al. (2009). *Assisting students struggling with mathematics: Response to intervention (RtI) for elementary and middle schools* (NCEE 2009–4060). Washington, DC: National Center for Education Evaluation and Regional Assistance. Accessed at http://ies.ed.gov/ncee/wwc/publications/practiceguides on July 25, 2011.

Gewertz, C. (2005). Training focuses on teachers' expectations. *Education Week, 24,* 30. Accessed at www.edweek.org/ew/articles/2005/04/06/30tesa.h24.html on April 18, 2011.

Goldsmith, L. (2001). Spheres of influence: Supporting mathematics education reform. *NASSP Bulletin, 3,* 53–61.

Good, C., & Dweck, C. S. (2006). A motivational approach to reasoning, resilience, and responsibility. In R. J. Sternberg & R. F. Subotnik (Eds.), *Optimizing student success in school with the other three Rs* (pp. 39–56). Greenwich, CT: Information Age.

Grant, C. M., & Davenport, L. R. (2009). Principals in partnership with math coaches. *Principal Magazine, 88*(5), 36–41.

Grant, C. M., Nelson, B. S., Weinberg, A. S., Sassi, A., Davidson, E., & Holland, S. G. B. (2006). *Lenses on learning supervision: Focusing on mathematical thinking—facilitator book.* Parsippany, NJ: Seymour.

Haycock, K. (2009). *Statement on the 2009 NAEP mathematics results.* Accessed at www.edtrust.org /dc/press-room/press-release/statement-on-the-2009-naep-mathematics-results on July 25, 2011.

Haycock, K. (2011). *NAEP 2009 transcript study.* Accessed at www.edtrust.org/dc/press-room /press-release/statement-by-kati-haycock-on-naep-2009-high-school-transcript-study on July 25, 2011.

Hembree, R., & Dessart, D. (1986). Effects of hand-held calculators in pre-college mathematics education: A meta-analysis. *Journal for Research in Mathematics Education, 17*(2), 83–89.

Henningson, M., & Stein, M. K. (1997). Mathematical tasks and student cognition: Classroom based factors that support and inhibit high-level mathematical thinking and reasoning. *Journal for Research in Mathematics Education, 29,* 524–549.

Hiebert, J., & Grouws, D. A. (2007). The effects of classroom teaching on students' learning. In F. K. Lester Jr. (Ed.), *Second handbook of research on mathematics teaching and learning* (pp. 371–404). Charlotte, NC: Information Age.

Individuals with Disabilities Education Improvement Act, 20 U.S.C. § 1400 (2004).

Jensen-Sheffield, L. (Ed.). (1999). *Developing mathematically promising students.* Reston, VA: National Council of Teachers of Mathematics.

Jeynes, W. H. (2005). *Parental involvement and student achievement: A meta-analysis* (Family Involvement Research Digest). Cambridge, MA: Harvard Family Research Project. Accessed at www.gse.harvard.edu/hfrp/publications_resources/publications_series/family_involvement _research_digests/parental_involvement_and_student_achievement_a_meta_analysis on July 25, 2011.

Kanold, T. (2007). Standards for the observation, supervision and improvement of mathematics teaching. In T. Martin (Ed.), *Mathematics teaching today: Improving practice, improving student learning* (2nd ed., pp. 65–78). Reston, VA: National Council of Teachers of Mathematics.

Kanold, T. (2011). *The five disciplines of PLC leaders.* Bloomington, IN: Solution Tree Press.

Kanter, P. F., & Darby, L. B. (1999). *Helping your child learn math.* Washington, DC: Author. Accessed at www.ed.gov/pubs/parents/Math on July 25, 2011.

Kober, N. (1991). *What we know about mathematics teaching and learning.* Washington, DC: Council for Educational Development and Research.

Lappan, G., & Briars, D. J. (1995). How should mathematics be taught? In I. Carl (Ed.), *75 years of progress: Prospects for school mathematics* (pp. 131–156). Reston, VA: National Council of Teachers of Mathematics.

Leinwand, S. (2009). *Accessible mathematics: 10 instructional shifts that raise student achievement.* Portsmouth, NH: Heinemann.

Lester, F. K., Jr. (Ed.). (2007). *Second handbook of research on mathematics teaching and learning.* Charlotte, NC: Information Age.

Loucks-Horsley, S., Love, N., Stiles, K. E., Mundry, S., & Hewson, P. W. (2003). *Designing professional development for teachers of science and mathematics* (2nd ed.). Thousand Oaks, CA: Corwin Press.

Marzano, R. J. (2003). *Classroom management that works.* Alexandria, VA: Association for Supervision and Curriculum Development.

Marzano, R. J., & Pickering, D. J. (2011). *The highly engaged classroom.* Bloomington, IN: Marzano Research Laboratory.

Math & Science Collaborative. (2005). *Mathematics standards in Pittsburgh's public schools: A parent's handbook, grades 6–8.* Homestead, PA: Author.

Mathematical Sciences Education Board. (1993). *Measuring what counts: A conceptual guide for mathematics assessment.* Washington, DC: National Academies Press.

Mazzocco, M. M. M. (2007). Defining and differentiating mathematical learning disabilities and difficulties. In D. Berch & M. M. M. Mazzocco (Eds.), *Why is math so hard for some children? The nature and origins of mathematics learning difficulties and disabilities* (pp. 29–47). Baltimore: Brookes.

McKellar, D. (2007). *Math doesn't suck!* Hudson, NY: Hudson Street Press.

Mizell, H. (2010). *Why professional development matters.* Oxford, OH: Learning Forward.

Mueller, C. M., & Dweck, C. S. (1998). Intelligence praise can undermine motivation and performance. *Journal of Personality and Social Psychology, 75,* 33–52.

National Assessment of Educational Progress. (1992). NAEP questions tool: Grade 4, block M7, question 10. Accessed at http://nces.ed.gov/nationsreportcard/itmrlsx/detail .aspx?subject=mathematics on July 25, 2011.

National Assessment of Educational Progress. (2007). NAEP questions tool: Grade 4, block M9, question 18. Accessed at http://nces.ed.gov/nationsreportcard/itmrlsx/detail .aspx?subject=mathematics on July 25, 2011.

National Board for Professional Teaching Standards. (2011). *Middle childhood generalist standards (for teachers of students ages 7–12)* [Draft]. Arlington, VA: Author.

National Council of Supervisors of Mathematics. (2008a). *Improving student achievement in mathematics for students with special needs* (Position Paper No. 4). Denver: Author.

National Council of Supervisors of Mathematics. (2008b). *The PRIME leadership framework: Principles and indicators for mathematics education leaders.* Bloomington, IN: Solution Tree Press.

National Council of Supervisors of Mathematics. (2009). *Improving student achievement in mathematics by addressing the needs of English language learners* (Position Paper No. 6). Denver: Author.

National Council of Supervisors of Mathematics. (2010). *Improving student achievement in mathematics by systematically integrating effective technology* (Position Paper No. 8). Accessed www.mathedleadership.org/docs/resources/positionpapers/NCSMPositionPaper8.pdf on July 25, 2011.

National Council of Teachers of Mathematics. (1989). *Curriculum and evaluation standards for school mathematics.* Reston, VA: Author.

National Council of Teachers of Mathematics. (2000). *Principles and standards for school mathematics.* Reston, VA: Author.

National Council of Teachers of Mathematics. (2006). *Curriculum focal points for prekindergarten through grade 8 mathematics: A quest for coherence.* Reston, VA: Author.

National Council of Teachers of Mathematics. (2007). *Research clips: What is formative assessment?* Reston, VA: Author

National Council of Teachers of Mathematics. (2008). *Equity in mathematics education—position statement.* Reston, VA: Author.

National Council of Teachers of Mathematics. (2010). *Making it happen: A guide to interpreting and implementing common core state standards for mathematics.* Reston, VA: Author.

National Education Association. (2008). *Changing role of school leadership* (Policy Brief No. 9). Washington, DC: Author.

National Education Association. (n.d.). *A parent's guide to helping your child with today's math* [Brochure]. Washington, DC: Author.

National Mathematics Advisory Panel. (2008). *Foundations for success: The national mathematics report.* Washington, DC: U.S. Department of Education.

National Research Council. (1999). *How people learn: Brain, mind, experience and school.* Washington, DC: National Academies Press.

National Research Council. (2001). *Adding it up: Helping children learn mathematics.* Washington, DC: National Academies Press.

National Staff Development Council. (2008). Professional development, defined for law. *Journal of Staff Development, 29*(3), 6.

Nelson, B. S., & Sassi, A. (2006). What to look for in your math classrooms. *Principal Magazine,* November/December, 46–49.

Neuman, M., & Mohr, N. (2001). Cracking the mathematics and science barrier: Principles for principals. *NASSP Bulletin, 85*(623), 43–52.

Nolan, J., & Francis, P. (1992). Changing perspectives in curriculum and instruction. In C. D. Glickman (Ed.), *Supervision in transition: The 1992 ASCD yearbook* (pp. 44–60). Alexandria, VA: Association for Supervision and Curriculum Development.

Pashler, H., Bain, P., Bottge, B., Graesser, A., Koedinger, K., McDaniel, M., et al. (2007). *Organizing instruction and study to improve student learning* (NCER 2007–2004). Washington, DC: National Center for Education Research, Institute of Education Sciences, U.S. Department of Education. Accessed at http://ies.ed.gov/ncee/wwc/pdf/practiceguides/20072004.pdf on July 25, 2011.

Popham, J. (2006). All about accountability: Phony formative assessments: Buyer beware! *Educational Leadership, 64*(3), 86–87.

Public Agenda Foundation. (1993). *Math leads the way: Perspectives on math reform.* Arlington, VA: Author.

Ramani, G. B., & Siegler, R. S. (2008). Promoting broad and stable improvements in low-income children's numerical knowledge through playing number board games. *Child Development, 79,* 375–394.

Reeves, D. (2007). Challenges and choices: The role of educational leaders in effective assessment. In D. Reeves (Ed.), *Ahead of the curve: The power of assessment to transform teaching and learning* (pp. 227–252). Bloomington, IN: Solution Tree Press.

Reinhart, S. (2000). Never say anything a kid can say. *Mathematics Teaching in the Middle School, 5*(8), 478–483.

Resnick, L. (Ed.). (2006). Do the math: Cognitive demand makes a difference. *American Education Research Association, 4*(2), 1–4. Accessed at www.aera.net/uploadedFiles/Journals_and _Publications/Research_Points/RP_Fall06.pdf on July 25, 2011.

Reys, B., & Fennell, F. (2003). Who should lead instruction at the elementary level? *Teaching Children Mathematics, 9,* 277–282.

Sarama, J., & Clements, D. H. (2009). *Early childhood mathematics education research: Learning trajectories for young children.* New York: Routledge.

Schmoker, M. (2005). Here and now: Improving teaching and learning. In R. DuFour, R. Eaker, & R. DuFour (Eds.), *On common ground: The power of professional learning communities* (pp. xi–xvi). Bloomington, IN: Solution Tree Press.

School-Home Links. (2001). *Research: Family involvement and student achievement.* Accessed at www .schoolhomelinks.com/research2.html on January 12, 2011.

Siegler, R., Carpenter, T., Fennell, F., Geary, D., Lewis, J., Okamoto, Y., et al. (2010). *Developing effective fractions instruction for kindergarten through 8th grade: A practice guide.* Washington, DC: National Center for Education Evaluation and Regional Assistance. Accessed at http://ies .ed.gov/ncee/wwc/publications/practiceguides on July 25, 2011.

Smith, M. S., Bill, V., & Hughes, E. K. (2008). Thinking through a lesson: Successfully implementing high-level tasks. *Mathematics Teaching in the Middle School, 14*(3), 132–138.

Smith, M. S., & Stein, M. K. (1998). Mathematical tasks as a framework for reflection: From research to practice. *Mathematics Teaching in the Middle School, 3*(4), 268–275.

Smith, M. S., & Stein, M. K. (2011). *5 practices for orchestrating productive mathematics discussions.* Reston, VA: National Council of Teachers of Mathematics.

Sowder, J. T. (2007). The mathematics education and development of teachers. In F. K. Lester Jr. (Ed.), *Second handbook of research on mathematics teaching and learning* (pp. 186–215). Charlotte, NC: Information Age.

Sparks, D. (2002). *Designing powerful professional development for teachers and principals.* Oxford, OH: National Staff Development Council.

Spillane, J. P. (2005). Primary school leadership practice: How the subject matters. *School Leadership and Management, 25*(4), 383–397.

Stein, M. K., Engle, R., Smith, M., & Hughes, E. (2008). Orchestrating productive mathematical discussions: Five practices for helping teachers move beyond show and tell. *Mathematical Thinking and Learning, 10*(4), 313–340.

Stiggins, R. (2002). Assessment crisis: The absence of assessment FOR learning. *Phi Delta Kappan, 83*(10), 758–765.

Stiggins, R. (2007). Assessment *for* learning: An essential function of productive instruction. In D. Reeves (Ed.), *Ahead of the curve: The power of assessment to transform teaching and learning* (pp. 59–78). Bloomington, IN: Solution Tree Press.

Stiggins, R., Arter, J., Chappuis, J., & Chappuis, S. (2006). *Classroom assessment for student learning: Doing it right—Using it well.* Princeton, NJ: Educational Testing Service.

Stigler, J., & Hiebert, J. (1999). *The teaching gap.* New York: The Free Press.

Swafford, J. O., & Brown, C. A. (1989). Attitudes. In M. M. Lindquist (Ed), *Results from the fourth mathematics assessment of the National Assessment of Educational Progress* (pp. 106–116). Reston, VA: National Council of Teachers of Mathematics.

Swan, M. (2005). *Improving learning in mathematics: Challenges and strategies.* Cheshire, England: Department for Education and Skills Standards Unit.

Tate, W., & Rousseau, C. (2007). Engineering change in mathematics education: Research policy and practice. In F. K. Lester Jr. (Ed.), *Second handbook of research on mathematics teaching and learning* (pp. 1209–1246). Charlotte, NC: Information Age.

Tyler, R. (1950). *Basic principles of curriculum and instruction.* Chicago: University of Chicago Press.

U.S. Department of Education. (1998). Partners in learning: How schools can support family involvement in education. In *Partnership for family involvement.* Accessed at www.ed.gov/pubs/PFIE/schools.html on August 24, 2011.

U.S. Department of Education. (2004). *Helping your child learn mathematics.* Washington, DC: Author.

Weiss, I. R., & Pasley, J. D. (2004). What is high-quality instruction? *Educational Leadership, 61*(5), 24–28.

Weiss, I. R., Pasley, J. D., Smith, P. S., Banilower, E. R., & Heck, D. J. (2003). *Looking inside the classroom: A study of K–12 mathematics and science education in the United States.* Chapel Hill, NC: Horizon Research.

Wiliam, D. (2007a). Content *then* process: Teacher learning communities in the service of formative assessment. In D. Reeves (Ed.), *Ahead of the curve: The power of assessment to transform teaching and learning* (pp. 183–206). Bloomington, IN: Solution Tree Press.

Wiliam, D. (2007b). Keeping learning on track: Classroom assessment and the regulation of learning. In F. K. Lester Jr. (Ed.), *Second handbook of research on mathematics teaching and learning* (pp. 1051–1098). Charlotte, NC: Information Age.

Wiliam, D., Lee, C., Harrison, C., & Black, P. (2004). Teachers developing assessment for learning: Impact on student achievement. *Assessment in Education: Principles, Policy and Practice, 11*(1), 49–65.

Wood, T. (2001). Teaching differently: Creating opportunities for learning mathematics [Special issue]. *Theory Into Practice, 40*(2), 110–117.

INDEX

The PRIME Leadership Framework
PRinciples and Indicators for Mathematics Education Leaders
National Council of Supervisors of Mathematics (NCSM)
Every leader in K–12 mathematics education should own this book. It reveals four leadership principles and twelve action indicators essential to creating equity and excellence in math programs. The NCSM leadership framework for dialogue and collaborative action includes reproducibles, reflective questions, and additional resources.
BKF250

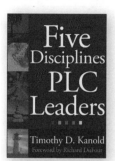

The Five Disciplines of PLC Leaders
Timothy D. Kanold
Foreword by Richard DuFour
Effective leadership in a professional learning community requires practice, patience, and skill. Through engaging examples and accessible language, this book offers a focused framework that will help educators maintain balance and consistent vision as they strengthen the skills of PLC leadership.
BKF495

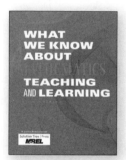

What We Know About Mathematics Teaching and Learning
McREL
Designed for accessibility, this book supports mathematics education reform and brings the rich world of education research and practice to preK–12 educators. It asks important questions, provides background research, offers implications for improving classroom instruction, and lists resources for further reading.
BKF395

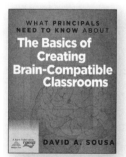

What Principals Need to Know About the Basics of Creating Brain-Compatible Classrooms
David A. Sousa
Understand the basics for creating a brain-compatible classroom with this brief, accessible guide customized for principals. This book provides an overview of educational neuroscience designed to help principals construct meaningful professional development that enhances teachers' knowledge and skills about brain-compatible learning.
BKF463

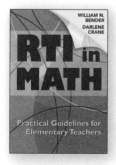

RTI in Math
Practical Guidelines for Elementary Teachers
William N. Bender and Darlene Crane
Explore common student difficulties in math and see a three-tier RTI model in action. The authors provide an overview of research, detailed guidance through each stage of implementation, tools for reflection and growth, and discussion of support strategies beyond the classroom.
BKF279

Solution Tree | Press   *a division of* Solution Tree   Visit solution-tree.com or call 800.733.6786 to order.